Re-imagining the Parish

Re-imagining the Parish

Base Communities, Adulthood, and Family Consciousness

Patrick J. Brennan

CROSSROAD · NEW YORK

1990

The Crossroad Publishing Company
370 Lexington Avenue, New York, NY 10017

Copyright © 1990 by Patrick J. Brennan

Printed in the United States of America

Library of Congress Cataloging-in-Publication Data

Brennan, Patrick J.
    Re-imagining the parish : base communities, adulthood, and family
consciousness / Patrick J. Brennan.
        p.   cm.
    Includes bibliographical references.
    ISBN 0-8245-1002-X
    1. Basic Christian communities.   2. Christian education of adults.
3. Church work with families—Catholic Church.   4. Family—Religious
life.   I. Title.
BX2347.7.B74   1990
250—dc20   89-29311
                                                                      CIP

To William and Helen (Canty) Brennan,
My Parents,

Pastors of a Small Christian Community for 38 years
at 7937 South Fairfield, Chicago

. . . who have become a shrine in my heart

Contents

17. The Faith Community as Training Center for Parenting   132

18. Family-Centered Evangelization and Catechesis   137

19. So Now . . .   141

        Appendix   145

        Bibliography   147

Introduction

Being a Chicago-born Irish Catholic, *the parish* is one of the loves of my life. Even if I were not an ordained minister, my personal spirituality would motivate me to be highly invested in the parish in which I would reside. Only the most naïve among us would not admit that the parish, in its status quo form, as we have known it for the past thirty or forty years, is not as effective in passing on and celebrating faith as it once was. While still "the place where the action is," when it comes to spirituality and faith, the parish is experiencing difficulties: a shortage of priests and religious; a significant number of so-called believers who no longer worship or relate to a faith community; others who are only minimally involved in the parish comunity via Mass attendance; a misguided young adult population often motivated more by wallet than conscience; a great unevenness among congregations and celebrants in the quality of liturgy; and school and CCD programs that seem to fail in achieving their mission.

This book is based on a conviction: *that the parish many of us knew and loved as we grew up is inadequate to meet the evangelical needs of believers in the future.* Though Vatican II vocabulary resounds through our parishes, and though many parishes have experienced an explosion of lay ministries, often the paradigm for parish remains basically the same as it was for our grandparents: child-centered school and CCD programs and organizations. This model or paradigm, institutionalized almost a century ago, simply is not as effective as it once was, amid the significant social changes that our age has witnessed.

So I offer the thoughts in this book as seminal ideas about re-imagining the parish around key elements different from school, CCD, and the kind of lay volunteer ministries so popular in our day. The three lenses for future parish life that I am advocating are: *small intentional communities,* an emphasis on *adult faith formation,* and an expanded *family consciousness* in parish ministries.

After a conference recently in Houston, at which I was advocating these "new lenses," someone approached me and said, "You are too much of a *warrior,* trying to make these things happen. Play the role of the *magician.* Through the power of the Holy Spirit these three realities are happening already. The magician, through slight of hand, convinces others that he had a role in its coming to be." I think my critic was on target. The three values I am advocating in this book are happening, breaking into reality already—through the grace of God. If the synthesis of material in this book helps a little to facilitate the mystery, the process, I will be pleased "with my slight of hand."

I want to thank Father Tim O'Connell, director of the Institute of Pastoral Studies of Loyola University of Chicago, who trusted me enough to allow me to teach on these "new lenses" for parish, and so bring some clarity and cohesion to my own vision. Special thanks to Michael Leach, who suggested that I write this book, and also Gene Gollogly and Robert Heller of *Crossroad,* for their trust in the concepts behind this book, and their patience in waiting for the text. Thanks also to Dawn Mayer, valued friend and co-worker, whose editorial, typing, and supportive skills have made this book possible.

Part I

Base Communities

1

On Imagining and Re-imagining

For years, when I heard people in religious education or pastoral ministry talk about imagination, and the primacy of imagination, I immediately had negative connotations about the word. Imagination: it spoke to me of fantasy, the unreal, something for children. In recent years I have come to see imagination in a new light. Imagination does not focus on what we traditionally call the *imaginary*. Everyone has imagination; and it is the deposit or container of that which we value the most in life, or deem important in life. Our imaginations fire us up, to rise from bed in the morning. We dream out of our imagination at night.

What is this often ignored, unpondered reality that we call imagination? On one level, imagination refers to one's abilities in hunching or intuition. In imagining, the mind jumps. One has flashes of insight, sees things, dreams in a frequently unordered, irrational way. With imagining, a person often has a flash of an answer before he or she has the question. Great scientific discoveries are often flashes of the imagination before they are scientific discoveries. In science, we often set out to prove what we have already imagined. On one level imagination refers to nonsequential flashes of insight, wisdom, intuition—the jumping of the mind to something new, something possible but never seen or understood before.

There is another level of meaning to imagination. It refers more specifically to dreaming. Robert Kennedy often described himself as a person who "dreamed dreams and asked 'why not'?" The great visionaries of history—the Kennedys, Martin Luther King, Jr., Gandhi, the prophets, some of the saints, Jesus—all are examples of human beings who exercised well the dreaming function of imagination. Though there can be a down side or demonic edge to imaginative dreaming—for example, the imaginative dreaming of Jim Jones, Charles Manson, or Adolf Hitler—

imaginative dreaming has also been the wellspring of great, bold new visions for the world and societies. Imagination gives birth to new ages of the human family and new levels of human consciousness. The new age of the reign of God, or the kingdom of God, which is the overarching metaphor that summarizes the ministry and preaching of Jesus, was a function of the imagination, not only of Jesus but also of the imaginations of many of his Jewish predecessors who felt they lived on the threshold of a new age, that would be counter-cultural, God-centered, and consist of renewed styles of relating to each other as men and women, brothers and sisters.

Imagination functions in flashes of insight and intuition. Imagination gives birth to dreams that become scientific discoveries, political realities, altered styles of relating, and religious or spiritual or cultural transformation. Imagination refers to something else, hinted at earlier. Consider television advertising. A beer commercial recently portrayed a young man in his early twenties staring into the camera. He said:

"I believe in racquet ball!" The scene flashes to the young man apparently winning over his opponent on a court.

"I believe in fast cars!" The camera next flashes to the young man exercising great authority over a flashy, speeding sports car.

"I believe in my girl friend!" We next see him with an attractive young woman, with obvious sex appeal.

The final scene shows the man holding a can of beer, which apparently holds a mystical fascination for him. "And I believe in Brand X," he says. The scene fades to a script: "Brand X Beer: A Beer You Can Believe In!"

In thirty-five seconds, viewers' imaginations are penetrated and influenced by this ad. A simple beer commercial offers images that in effect tell persons what is important in life, what they ought to be concerned about. In this specific ad, the images of competition (in racquet ball), fast and flashy cars, sexual attractiveness and activity, and a mind-altering substance, alcohol, are offered as images worth noting, paying attention to, and are in fact realities on which one could build a life.

Notice also the primary verb used, I believe. The root meaning of *credo* did not, centuries ago, refer to intellectual consent. It originally meant: *I give my heart to.* The advertising of consumer society in a real sense evangelizes us toward, tells us, what we should give our hearts to. We are offered images through which we are to view life, with which we are to live life.

When I said earlier that we live and dream out of our imaginations, I was referring to how we all live out of dominant images. All advertising—on another level, evangelization—is an attempt to influence persons' dominant images, to influence what they value, what they hold sacred, what they think is important.

Conversion, Transformation, and the Imagination

When a person goes through a process or series of events called conversion or spiritual transformation, it is the imagination that is being most influenced. Later on in the process, the intellect may kick in to try to rationalize—in a positive sense—as well as understand and name the dynamics that are occurring. But the most alive and active force in the conversion process is the imagination. In the midst of conversion, my dominant images, the lens with which I view life, the meaning system that I have created, my sense of what is important in life, my values—these are the things that begin to shift. Often such moments and periods are quite painful, because what the person involved is experiencing is a shaking of the imagination, often a falling apart of the system with which one interpreted life, or a felt sense of how impoverished one's dominant images have been, how they no longer work or function in helping one live with meaning or purpose.

Often in the counseling office, I hear mid-life men who have given their hearts largely to their jobs, coming to grips with how empty their living for work has become. They are experiencing an image or paradigm shift, from the primacy of work to the importance, in many cases, of intimacy. I hear single women, in their thirties, speak of how they have given their hearts to career, and now feel an urge for marriage and family. These are examples of dominant image shift on the apparent level. Beneath the appearances of things there is often also a spiritual transformation occuring. The very human transitional experience can be a trigger experience for a more profound shift in the imagination.

In Christian conversion, a person experiences a shift from personally created or appropriated dominant images, or images offered to us by the consumer culture around us, to the dominant images of Jesus. As mentioned earlier, Jesus used the metaphor of the kingdom of God or the reign of God to summarize and communicate these dominant images. Among the dominant images of Jesus are: equality among persons; prophetic action against personal and systemic evil; mercy; forgiveness; justice;

prayerfulness; the loving parenthood of God; the cosmic power of the Holy Spirit; the salvific influence of Jesus' paschal mystery; the mystery of life, death, and resurrection going on in each of our lives; and the need for the centrality of God in one's life to achieve meaning and purpose.

Most typically a person cannot experience the shift from one's personal dominant images, or the consumer culture's dominant images, without help. Before my imagination can or will make the jump to the risky images of Jesus, I need to see his dominant images helping, working in the life of another person. Conversion, transformation, the shifting of dominant images demands the influence of a mentoring person or persons. Such persons pastor or shepherd us toward that jump of the imagination that leads to new life-giving images.

It should be noted that we cannot help but be mentored. Some force is always reaching for our imagination with claims to be *the truth, the direction* that we ought to be headed in. If we are not being mentored toward images of the kingdom of God, then some other system or set of images is holding our imagination, firing our imagination, directing our lives.

Life is a series of shifts of dominant images, a series of mentoring relationships that influence the direction of our lives, a series of breaking apart and coming together experiences. A person of faith gradually learns to trust the inevitability of the process, and the usually healthy, integral place that the process leads us to. A person of faith names the power or energy force present or at work in the process: it is the Spirit; it is grace.

To sum up, the imagination is the wellspring of our outlook, our vision, our priorities, what we think is important. The imagination is a network of dominant images that energize or motivate us. If the images are truly dysfunctional, they can actually restrict or narrow our energy and resources rather than animate us. Many forces converge to pattern and repattern our imaginations. One force is the power of Jesus and the gospel. The reign of God is a metaphor for the dominant images of Jesus. He did not come to these images solely on his own. Rather, he purified and enriched the reign of God imagery existent in Old Testament times. Christian conversion or transformation is the repatterning of the imagination with the dominant images of Jesus. It often is a painful process involving the breaking down of the status quo images that we have become comfortable or complacent with. The breaking down prompts the risky jumping of the imagination toward the imagery of Jesus. The whole process is difficult without mentoring persons, who often have made such a jump already. In shared faith, prayer, and modeling, they give us a glimpse of a possible new world, a new age, a new way of doing life.

Dominant Image Shifts on the Ecclesial Level

Not just individuals but also groups go through the process of image shifts. Later in this book, we will discuss stages that small groups or household churches go through as they relate together over the passage of time. On a broader scale, societies or cultures can experience dominant image shift. Politically, the American Revolution and the Russian Revolution were movements away from a monarchical lens for viewing a nation to a democratic and socialistic-communist lens. The transition from the nineteenth to the twentieth century saw many societies move from agrarian images to industrial images, for self-understanding and communication. Today, in terms of primary relationships, technological society is seriously threatening a communal understanding of society based on relationship, family, and neighborhood.

The shifting of dominant images happens also as organized religions, or churches, try to explain their identity and present themselves to the world. The first Christians imagined themselves as the dawning of a new, final age of humankind. Many felt the second coming of Christ was imminent. They imagined the church to be highly relational, consisting of families and networks of families and individuals sharing word, worship, and resources with each other. Gradually the church re-imagined itself around the dominant images of the political governing structures of the day. So hierarchy, monarchy, and pomp replaced the communal imagery of an earlier day. The Pauline image of the Mystical Body of Christ, popularized again earlier in this century, attempted to soften the hierarchical imagery, institutionalized by the Council of Trent. Vatican II did much to retrieve the horizontal, relationally-rooted imagery of the people of God of the original Christian movement. John Paul II's admonition in his encyclical *Redemptor Hominis* that we as church see ourselves as a *community of disciples* is a further refining of heavily relational imagining about church.

The most important point to keep in mind is this: whoever, whatever, we imagine ourselves to be, as individuals, as groups, as church, so also will we act. Imagination, and the firing of dominant images, always dictates behavior or action. This book, which encourages a rethinking of parish ministry around the spiritual formation of adults, ministry with a family consciousness, and the genesis of small, intentional communities, is obviously an appeal for an ecclesial dominant image shift from the trappings of a tridentine church, to another primordial set of images.

2

Ecclesiology—Vision
Influencing Praxis

I am amazed, as I work with parish staffs, how everyone comes with an ecclesiology or vision of what church is about. Often staffs are paralyzed, unable to work with each other productively. At first glance, it appears that there are personal conflicts between and among staff members. Closer scrutiny and listening to a little more dialogue between and among them reveals a deeper, more subtle, difficulty: ecclesiological conflicts. Often such conflicts are unnamed, in fact may be unconscious—"we just know we disagree with each other."

Ecclesiology is an all-pervasive reality. What a person feels about church, the raison d'être of church, is intimately related to one's understanding of the mystery of revelation, or God's self-manifestation. Similarly, ecclesiology dictates one's approach to ministry, one's sense of authority and leadership within church. Ecclesiology even influences how, or the style with which, one may lead prayer, or preside over worship. Ecclesiology certainly influences one's sacramental theology, as well as one's christology, or vision of the role of Christ in the cosmos.

The ecclesiology still in the marrow of the bones of clergy members, religious, and laity is the vertical ecclesiology articulated and institutionalized by the Council of Trent and other councils leading up to it. Vertical, traditionalistic ecclesiology very much sees church as an end onto itself. It is mother and teacher; it is the city of God here on earth. It is a society and culture within the societies and cultures of the world. It in many ways finds itself at variance with the world. Liberation theologian Leonardo Boff deliberately uses the word *traditionalistic* to describe this vision of church. He feels that there was a truly traditional ecclesiology

9

that certainly predated tridentine ecclesiology. It is my experience that
traditionalistic ecclesiology is still the dominant ecclesiology of our age.
Though we use the language of renewal, and speak the language of Vatican
II, the vision of church articulated in the Middle Ages still dominates. In
it a caste system of ontologically special, unique males determine the
direction of the universal body of the church. The bishop, representing the
pontiff in local churches, is in effect cloned in parishes in the diocese.
Priests, dwindling in number, create an elite group of trained professionals
that we call staff. This small coterie shares in some ways in the priests'
pastoring functions. The persons populating these staffs may all speak the
language of renewal but often are nothing more than nouveau clerics
perpetuating the system.

The system is alienating at root in that it flies in the face of baptismal
spirituality and healthy sacramental theology, which teach us that someone who has been fully initiated into the church, immersed in the body of
Christ, fed regularly by word and sacrament, by nature ought also to be
engaged in the apostolate or mission of the church. There cannot be *a few*
who minister. All initiated Christians ought to belong to evangelizing,
ministering congregations. With the right and power to minister re-
stricted to a few in high positions in a hierarchical pattern, the ordinary
believer is rendered a consumer, the receiver of ministerial services.
Traditionalistic ecclesiology has created a consumer church. In this consumer church, God's people are being inadequately pastored, shepherded,
mentored—leaving their imagination quite open to be mentored by
consumer culture, or by cults, sects, or fundamentalistic or evangelical
churches, who build on the power of the unleashed ordinary Christian, the
empowered individual and congregation.

The ecclesiology the church currently seems locked into sees church as
an end in itself. Avery Dulles reflected on this several years ago in *A Church
to Believe In*. He commented that the model of church that still dominates
most peoples' consciousness is that of the *institution*. Other "ologies" are
always connected to such an existential, if unpondered, ecclesiology.
Connected with this ecclesiology is a christology that explains how Jesus
came to found the institutional, hierarchical church. This ecclesiology has
a missiology, or vision of mission, attached to it—namely, that this one,
medieval vision of church is to be spread through the world; that indeed it
is that which will make us catholic, whole, one, universal.

There is an implicit theory of revelation in this ecclesiology also—
namely, that God's self-manifestation comes largely through papal and

conciliar pronouncements—that is, the tradition of the church, in a very confined sense.

Traditionalistic ecclesiology also reaches into sacramentology. Holy orders empowers one for priesthood; only male, ordained priests can preside at the eucharist. When they do, they are not so much presiders with an evangelizing, ministering community, or overseers of the many *koinonias* and household churches coming together. They are experienced more as the only persons with the ontological power to make Jesus really present in the assembly.

The church, renewed and refurbished on the apparent level by documents and councils, remains as described in the *lived* experience of many Catholics. It is a safe, comfortable, if not infantile church for those who attend it. It is a moribund church for others; it alienates, fails to motivate, and becomes the occasion for lapsing into spiritual privatism or some other spiritual expression for others. The institutional church has taken one local ecclesiology, the ecclesiology of the church of Rome, and mandated it for all local churches. As stated earlier, it is at best a spiritualization of the Roman civil political system of a given age.

Toward a Renewed Ecclesiology

I hope the foregoing glimpse of the relationship between ecclesiology and christology, missiology, sacramentology, and vision of revelation makes at least one thing apparent: as one *imagines* church, so one does, lives, behaves as church. The dominant image dictates the praxis.

Liberation theologians like Jon Sobrino, Juan Segundo, Guillermo Cook, Gustavo Gutiérrez, Leonardo Boff, and others have been advocates for a renewed, cleansed ecclesiology, one with universal principles but also admitting of much cultural adaptation and syncretism (in a positive sense), that is, building on the local customs and symbols of people. Based on their experience with basic Christian communities, these writers have been advocating a *traditional* ecclesiology. A traditional ecclesiology, with roots in the first three centuries of Christianity, predates traditionalistic ecclesiology. It says of Catholic praxis that the people of God have been getting inadequate, if not poor, leadership. It advocates that the risen, cosmic Christ rightfully be restored as the leader of the universal movement that we call church. In their view, certainly the bishop of Rome serves a unitive, symbolic function for the church. But the only credible

leader of the church is the risen Christ. There are approximately 1.8
priests for every 10,000 Catholics in Brazil. In a spirit of pastoral honesty,
leaders there began to see over thirty years ago that pope, bishops, and
priests could not be seen as the center of church life. Even if vision
dictated such a structure, pragmatics would not allow it. No, in their
view, the risen Christ is at the center of every community—without him,
there is no real salvation, justice, holiness, or integrity of life.

If Christ is the supreme head of the church, what is the goal of the
church? Is the church an end in itself? No! In this more traditional view of
church, the church as movement, as people in a sacred relational bond of
faith, exists as servant and instrument of something larger, more important than itself—that is, the reign or kingdom of God.

The reign of God signals the dawning of a new age. The reign of God
introduces a new set of egalitarian, justice-oriented behaviors. The reign of
God is a people and a place. All of what has already been said about the
reign of God must be incarnated, made real, enfleshed by persons with
some bondedness to each other, in a given space, in a given moment of
time.

At least for liberation theologians, the reign of God breaks into situations of poverty; the reign of God is the special gift and experience of the
poor. Before God can become sovereign of a people's life, persons must
discover where they need the enrichment, the love, the meaning that only
God can bring. God has become poor in Christ and in the body of Christ
today. Church persons uncomfortable with the God who lives and reigns
in poverty must find a god and churches of power and might.

The impoverishment of traditionalistic ecclesiology is that it has not yet
found or named its locus of poverty. In fact, the reason American culture,
the American church, does and will have problems with a return to a
pretridentine ecclesiology is that we as a society are not in touch with our
societal poverty. With all our creature comforts and gadgetry, we often fail
to realize our need for each other, for relationships, and for God. In turn,
the truly impoverished in our ghettos, hypnotized by the "mythical its" of
the middle and upper classes, envision "the it" as that which will make
them happy. Thus, all strata of society pursue, in their own ways, the same
carrot, rather than confronting our universal poverty, our need for meaning, God, and love.

This older, more primitive version of ecclesiology also results in some
pragmatics. If the church exists as agent of the kingdom, all the baptized
are deacons, servants, and ministers of the kingdom. Ministry is rooted in
giftedness, in the placing of one's discerned charisms at the service of the

reign of God, which is becoming enfleshed in community. Missiology is not corraling the world into one vision of reality that dichotomizes sacred and secular. Rather, mission is to bring the reign of God into the marketplace, to facilitate the reign of God as it emerges in the world.

Traditional ecclesiology urges us to rethink revelation. Certainly key elements of revelation and truth have been captured in papal, credal, conciliar pronouncements. But renewed ecclesiolgy envisions revelation as ongoing in the lived experience of people in community. God spoke, yes; but God also *speaks* in the ongoing stories of peoples' lives. People of faith gather in community to discern the movement of God in their individual and communal lives.

This ecclesiology also prompts us to rethink sacraments. Is holy orders the sacrament that ordains men for priesthood, or one of many commissioning rituals that anoints persons for leadership in the Christian community, charismatic leaders who will bring order to the diverse ministries of the community? Is eucharist something ordained ministers make happen, or the memorial celebration of Christ's paschal victory, at which the word is broken open, the bread, the real presence of Christ, is broken and shared, and the people of God are commissioned to go and facilitate the actualization of the kingdom in the world? The rite of Christian initiation of adults (RCIA), in its 1988 revised form, challenges the church to completely rethink sacraments: moving from the "acquisition of holy things mind-set" to sacraments as vowing moments in the lifelong process of conversion. Baptism, confirmation, and eucharist are the beginning of immersion into the paschal mystery of Christ, and the beginning of one's responsibilities for the unfolding of the reign of God.

On Discipleship, *Ecclesia,* and *Koinonia*

A retrieving of traditional ecclesiology would certainly emphasize the central image of *discipleship* in its renewed understanding of church. John Paul II's *Redemptor Hominis* speaks of church as a community of disciples. Avery Dulles, in *A Church to Believe In,* claims that "the community of disciples" is the most fitting description of church, the most congruent with the early Christian experience.

If the church were to take the metaphor of God's reign seriously, it would certainly turn our experience of parish or faith community inside out. The same is true of the metaphor or lens of discipleship. The four evangelists tell us that Jesus spoke to *crowds,* but the *disciples* formed *smaller groups* who followed him, in community, privileged with special time with and teaching from the rabbi. There seems to have been another group, the *sympathizers,* who were not a parapatetic learning group, as the disciples were, but rather persons who *opened their homes* to Jesus for meals, gatherings, and discussions. We will see that the *sympathizers* may very well have laid the groundwork for the household churches of the first centuries of Christianity. Finally, there were the *apostles,* those sent to the world to be the representatives of the Lord to the world. Imagine a church or a parish made up of sympathizers, disciples, and apostles, all living with a sense of mission around the reign of God. The experience of church would indeed be a much more vital experience than that which we often experience today.

Disciples, sympathizers, and apostles need a church, or parish, that holds two values in tension—*ecclesia* and *koinonia. Ecclesia* refers to the large gatherings of the faithful that we most often experience at weekend worship. *Koinonia* refers to smaller units of the larger body; they gather around felt needs or some other common bond, to pray, share life, and break open God's word from Scripture. *Ecclesia* is inadequate for living the spirituality and ecclesiology discussed as "traditional," rather than "traditionalistic." *Ecclesia* often makes persons consumers, observers, anonymous to each other. In larger, American suburban parishes, references to the parish as "community" are so much jargon. Eucharist often is a gathering of strangers, who are there to take, consume: a homily, the bread and wine—and the Sunday paper.

Ecclesia can be a heartfelt experience, a meaningful experience, if wedded to *koinonia,* genuine experiences, on a regular basis, of the essence of church. Bernard Lee and Michael Cowan, in their book *Dangerous Memories,* name the following as the core experiences of what church is most about: *kerygma* (sharing the word), *leitourgia* (prayer and worship), *diakonia* (service, ministry), and *koinonia* (shared fellowship). These four dynamics of church need to be experienced in a small Christian community before and as they are experienced in the *ecclesia* or large church.

In *koinonia* there is both *accountability* and *responsibility* around the dynamics of word, prayer, service, and fellowship. In *ecclesia* there may not be that accountability or responsibility. Persons can literally hide, divorced and alienated from each other—anonymous to each other. The *kerygma, leitourgia,* and *diakonia* needed on the level of *ecclesia* needs to be recharged, renewed, on the smaller, cellular level of *koinonia.* This is what liberation theologians mean when they refer to the base community movement as the actual "cleansing" of the church on the cellular level.

Tempering a *Koinonia* Emphasis: A Broad Ecclesiology

The Catholic Church, universal and inclusive—in the ideal order—is at once a worldwide movement and family; a local expression, often called "local church," as it manifests itself as a diocese or archdiocese; a smaller gathering of believers called a parish; a small group or cell of believers called *koinonia,* or basic intentional ecclesial community; the domestic church of home or family. In frustration with a slow-moving institution, small groups—basic communities, or extended families—household churches sometimes threaten to or actually do split off from the other expressions of church—namely, the church universal, the diocese, or parish. As will, I hope, become more apparent in a later chapter, such a "congregational" type of movement is a violation of the best of Catholic ecclesiology. Connectedness is an indispensable element of healthy ecclesial praxis. Paul reflects on this in 1 Corinthians when he speaks of how the different members of the body of Christ are *indispensable* to each other, and ought not to say to other members of the body "we do not need you." Even if one of the members of the body is becoming problematic, that is not reason for amputation, or schism—rather, that problematic member is in need of more care from the rest of the members.

Leaving room, then, for prophetic critique and action on the part of small communities toward the larger body, it is vital for the small communities to stay connected to and in communication with parish, diocese, pastor, bishop—and to the degree possible—the leading shepherd, the pope. The person who personifies well this need for maintaining the interconnectedness of the various strata of church is Leonardo Boff—who, when silenced temporarily by the Vatican, assumed a posture of obedience rather than sever ties—for himself and others—with the larger one.

Let us pause for a brief interlude that reframes some of this theory in more practical, parish-based conversation. Our traditionalistic ecclesiology is robbing people of quality pastoral care. To return to Boff's *traditional* ecclesiology would alter our concept of pastoring.

3

Small Communities and Neighborhood Ministers: A Response to the Problems of Inadequate Pastoring

The title of this chapter may be misleading. I can only offer praise to the many fine men who labor in their parishes with great dedication and effectiveness. Rather I am addressing an ecclesiological problem in the chapter: there are so many sheep and not enough shepherds. This is one of the chief dilemmas in the rising number of inactive Catholics. Too many persons are looking to one person and his associates, the pastoral staff, for pastoring. These pastoring and shepherding functions need to be shared much more extensively if we as church are to deacon or serve the reign of God.

The Ministry Years

Being fortunate enough to study under Fathers Jack Shea and Gerry Egan in the late 1970s in a doctor of ministry program, I was deeply influenced in my approach to ministry. In the first years in my first assignment, I functioned a great deal as the direct deliverer of services to the people of God. I guess I will always need to do that to some degree, but Shea and Egan shared another vision. In addition to doing direct delivery, could priests/pastors/staffs see themselves anew as trainers or facilitators of ministry? The model of ministry that evolved in those D. Min. years was a shift from a vertical-hierarchical model (staff mem-

16

ber→parishioner) to a horizontal model (staff member trains a lay leader/ couple; together they develop a ministerial team or community that is focused on a target population). In this model ministry looks more like this: staff→lay leaders→ministerial team→target population.

I remember when I first studied this model I said to myself: "This approach requires a real conversion of visions, of systems, of people's expectations, of ecclesiologies, and of my own and many priests' hearts." Rather than posing a job-threat to priests, with people taking the priest's job, this vision of and strategy for ministry has given me a much richer experience of what it means to be a leader. Instead of solely being the direct service person, I am a teacher/trainer in the new seminary or school of discipleship that we call parish. In St. Hubert's, St. Albert's, St. John the Evangelist's, and St. Michael's—parishes that I have served in recent years, I have experienced that this approach to ministry effects what Norman Shawchuck suggests in the title of his book *Let My People Go*. The power of a ministering congregation is unleashed in this model. At St. Hubert's, St. Albert's, and St. John's this strategy has been applied to all dimensions of ministry: religious education, worship, pastoral care, youth. Governance boards have been established to coordinate the various ministries of the ministering congregation. At St. Hubert's, St. Albert's, and St. John's schools of ministry were established that (a) help people discern their gifts for ministry; (b) give all parish ministers an overall renewed theology of ministry; and (c) train people in the unique skills required for the ministry that they feel called to do.

A conviction that has arisen out of twelve years of working this way is this: I will not begin a ministry without developing lay leaders and a ministering team that will own that ministry. After a year or two, that ministry should need me as an ongoing resource person, spiritual director, or consultant. But the ministry is not mine! I should be able to be transferred tomorrow, and it would go on. The ministry is "owned" by the ministering team or community.

Beyond Volunteerism

Too often, ministry is experienced by parishioners as volunteering for tasks. Thomas O'Meara in *Theology of Ministry* speaks of a more profound reality. He writes that ministry is public activity done by a baptized follower of Jesus, using charisms of the Spirit present in each personality to help realize the kingdom or reign of God. At St. John's as well as St. Michael's, significant time is being given to the *discernment of charisms* with persons coming forward to ministry. Evelyn Eaton Whitehead in "Leadership and Power: A View from the Social Sciences," in *Leadership Ministry in Community,* volume six of the Alternative Futures for Worship series, challenges us to always keep the metaphor of "servant leadership" before us and the people of God. James Whitehead, in the same volume, says that enablement—empowerment models, like the one I proposed earlier—are examples of disciples becoming *stewards,* taking responsibility for the community, assuming leadership. The ministries explosion is the breaking down of the consumer church—that is, passive Sunday Catholics who take their homily and their ritual—and go home.

Beyond Programs to Community

If there has been a shift in my consciousness since assuming my role as director of the Office for Evangelization in Chicago, it has been away from ministerial programs and toward *communities in which diverse ministries take place.* Even in the horizontal model of ministry that I described earlier there is a kind of nouveau clericalism in which some "elite" members minister, but not all the baptized have as yet had such a ministerial awakening. Even with these ministerial programs of the 1970s and 80s, people are being inadequately shepherded or pastored. I am aware of three directions that are expanding the pastoring function to many more persons, so that, in turn, many more persons may be touched.

Basic Christian Communities

Small intentional communities gather either on a neighborhood basis, or around some other healthy self-interest (parenting, marriage, work, need for healing, etc.). Someone must serve as pastor or shepherd for these small groups. The shepherd also helps to surface other ministers who will lead in prayer, Scripture, and life sharing, ministry to each other, and social justice ministries. Father Art Baranowski from the diocese of Detroit has done excellent work at his parish, St. Elizabeth Seton, and has three books out on his style of sharing pastoring, published by St. Anthony Messenger Press. Father Michael Eivers, of St. Boniface in

Pembrooke Pines, Florida, also has re-imaged his parish around small communities and the sharing of pastoring. Both Art and Mike say that key to the process is networking the various groups and pastoral leaders/ministers with each other and with the pastor and staff. We will study their models later in the book.

The Domestic Church

As I listened at pastors' days in Chicago recently, I heard a general feeling that school and CCD religious education efforts seem to do little to alleviate the growing inactive-alienation problem—Catholics are not going to church, and are not contributing. It is time to begin to mandate family involvement at every level of childhood religious education. Systems need to be changed to better evangelize the family. In addition, the parochial school and parish religious education programs need to offer training in parenting and basic faith-sharing skills as well as marriage and family life enrichment, so that mothers and fathers can retrieve their rightful place as pastors, shepherds of the domestic church, the home, the basic cell of church. This area will also be discussed in depth later.

Home Visitation, the Calling Ministry, Neighborhood Ministry

At a recent training session on the south side of Chicago, someone left an anonymous note on the podium at break-time. The pastor had invited me to present some ideas on home visitation to a group of leadership parishioners. The note read: "You and the pastor seem to be trying to turn us into a group of Jehovah's Witnesses." I tried to respond to the challenge. It is not so much that we are becoming Jehovah's Witnesses; rather the Witnesses and other proactive evangelizing groups have retrieved and activated some of the things that we as Catholics have forgotten.

The roots of the Confraternity of Christian Doctrine movement can be traced back to a young priest, Castello de Castellano, who, in 1536, gathered together men and women in Milan, Italy, to conduct schools of Christian doctrine. They were called "the Company of Christian Doctrine." Under the influence of people like Angela Merci, Charles Boromeo, Pope Paul V, Robert Bellarmine, Francis de Sales, and others, the movement quickly spread throughout Europe. The movement spread to this country at the turn of the century. In addition to the obvious ministry of catechist in CCD, another vital ministry was the "fisher" or the home visitor. The role of the fisher was to connect the catechetical experiences children received and the larger life of the parish with individual families and homes. As CCD has evolved in this country, the role of the fisher fell into disuse. Perhaps only the Legion of Mary has kept alive some form of proactive reach-out and home visitation in the past decades.

The fishers of the CCD movement, the Legion of Mary visitation teams, have attempted to respond to the call of Jesus in Matthew 4:19: "come after me, and I will make you fishers of men and women." The impetus to begin home visitation efforts is not a competitive step or strategy to respond to the success of other evangelical movements. It is rather a return to some pastoral strategies that we have forgotten, that we have allowed to fall into disuse. To begin home-oriented hospitality efforts is to reclaim preevangelization, the evangelization style of the early catechumenal church. As many church fathers attest in their writings, reach-out, invitation to the Christian community, was done quite informally—in homes, the marketplace, shops, and places of work. Thus, the catechumenal model of church, the history of CCD, and the lonely and heroic efforts of the Legion of Mary are evidence that to return to some form of personalized evangelization is simply a reclaiming of our own heritage and roots.

George Gallup's latest study on the unchurched, *The Unchurched American, 1988,* reports a small increase (from a previous study done in 1978), from 41 to 44 percent (of over 2500 respondents), of persons describing themselves as unchurched. On the other hand, he also reports a jump from 60 to 66 percent of persons who claim to believe in or be committed to God. Gallup has named this situation "The Crisis of Believing vs. Belonging." The American "cocooning" syndrome, or in its more insidious form, fierce individualism and privatism, has bred a generation who claim belief but do not want to be "in relationship with" other believers. Gallup feels that none of the mainline Christian churches are making effective inroads into the evangelization of the unchurched. Four of his main recommendations to the mainline churches are:

1. Stress religious experience over the institutional model of church; help people experience God in their everyday experience.
2. Evangelize the family, not just children; more and more include parents in the faith formation of their children.

3. Provide opportunities where small groups can gather around prayer and Scripture.
4. Begin more intensive reach-out and invitation efforts to the unchurched.

Gallup's fourth recommendation implies some kind of personal, relational experience, like home visitation.

In Chicago different parishes are using home visitation ministers in different ways.

1. A cluster of parishes, in close proximity to each other, trained over one hundred callers to do a need discernment for the area. Programs flowed then from the articulated needs of people in their homes. This is a wonderful way to design pastoral and religious education programs, rather than simply ascribing needs to people. The weakness of the effort was that it only happened once. "One-shot calls" can boomerang, and create more of a negative effect than a positive one. Should the church listen, care, visit, just once? I recommended follow-up visits in my critique of the effort. A principle I learned from some Dutch Reformed evangelical leaders is: repetition of visits, invitations, hospitality is a key to effective evangelizing.

2. Some parishes have added home visits to preparation of families for children's sacramental moments. These visitors become the equivalent of sponsors for the family and the child. Father Jimmy Nolan of Dublin, Ireland, has created a video on his program called "Christian Friends." The Christian Friends are the sponsoring, home-visitation figures.

3. Other parishes around the country have used a "gradually personal" visitation effort. Reach-out is packaged as a several-year preevangelization effort. A first round of visits involves pamphleting every house in the parish with information about the parish and extending an invitation to the alienated or unchurched to a series of open houses at the parish. Those who attend the open houses are then sent some follow-up reading material on the parish and the church in general. A third step involves some personal home visitation that eventually leads the visitation minister to extend an invitation to the person(s) being visited to join the parish through a catechumenal journey, or reenter or reconcile with the community through a process of formation parallel to, but distinct from, the RCIA.

4. Many parishes have begun to make registration of newcomers much

more of a process of covenanting with the faith community rather than filling out a card with a parish secretary. In this model, a visit by the neighborhood minister is followed by some experience of education and formation regarding life in the parish, frequently culminating in a ritual of welcome at one of the weekend liturgies.

5. Being a Chicagoan, I favor this last model, maybe because it builds on our notorious political system in Chicago. I call it the "precinct captain" model or the neighborhood pastor model. St. Denis's on the south side of Chicago, St. Agatha's, an inner-city parish on the west side, St. Odilo's in Berwyn, Illinois, and St. Michael's in Orland Park (both suburbs of Chicago) are among some of the parishes piloting this model. The neighborhood pastor or minister is assigned a geographical piece of the parish, usually fifteen to twenty homes in his or her immediate area. They become known to neighbors, Catholic and non-Catholic, active Catholics, alienated or nonpracticing, unchurched, as the parish representative in the area.

These ministers "pastor" by regularly welcoming newcomers, visiting and checking on the needs and opinions of active, church-going parishioners; bonding in some way with the alienated and unchurched; notifying pastoral care ministers of the sick or shut-in of the area; harnessing the resources of the neighborhood to aid grieving, needy, or traumatized neighbors; saying good-bye to those moving; distributing printed material of upcoming events; and whatever else arises in the natural evolution of the ministry.

I favor the fifth model because it really is a move toward a re-imagining of the parish via the lens of shared pastoring or shepherding. It seems to be a perfect first step toward the more in-depth pastoring or shepherding that could take place in small, intentional communities.

A word or two should be added on training. Whichever of the above— or other—models for home visitation is employed, the training remains somewhat the same. An overview of evangelization is necessary at the outset to provide the *why*, or motivation for the ministry. The rest of the training is oriented *away* from the heavily scripted manipulative monologue of proselytizers and *toward* the skills for nonmanipulative dialogue that good ministry and evangelizing require. The rest of the sessions focus on:

1. human relations skills; how to listen
2. why people leave the church; the deep hurts that often are hiding

behind a negative event ("church stories"); the different types of alienated people that will be met

3. reconciling responses: how to respond nondefensively to mistaken generalizations about the church
4. bridging/networking skills: connecting people in need with civic or church resources that might respond to genuine needs
5. invitation skills: how to gently invite to active membership in the community
6. appropriate faith-witnessing skills: how to use one's own faith story, not as a weapon, but as a healing instrument
7. how to use the telephone effectively

There are other skills, but the above seem to be the most important. In all cases, home visitation ministers must never present themselves as the "inactive team," commissioned to seek out "the bad boys and bad girls." Training can be done in flex-type situations: six to eight evening sessions, or pieces of a weekend. Triadlike, laboratory practicing with each other is vital to this training. It must be joined to theoretical input.

Two books that I have written—*The Evangelizing Parish* and *The Reconciling Parish*—may be useful in getting started.

True ministerial enablement and empowerment mean sharing the shepherding, pastoring function broadly, with gifted people called to such ministry. Sharing pastoring requires a redefinition of who we are and what we do as priests or staff members. Balancing the budget and asbestos abatement must be given over to others gifted in such areas so that priests and other members of pastoral staffs can become enablers, spiritual directors, empowerers, mentors, and rabbis. God's people deserve better and more shepherding.

4

From Addiction to Transformation

In recent years, Dr. Gerald May, Anne Wilson Schaef, Diane Fassel, and others have been doing pioneering work in the area of addictions. The most important insight that all three have brought to light is that addiction is indeed a growing phenomenon in our society. The most obvious addictions are those to alcohol or drugs. In fact, the number of addictions in today's world abound. Addictions can be to substances, or to processes. Substance addictions are obvious: food, alcohol, drugs, caffeine, nicotine. Process addictions are more subtle. They include addictions to work, dysfunctional relationships, sex, worry, stress, and on and on. An addiction is essentially a relationship with anyone or anything that robs one of life. Addictions always end in death or destruction.

Another term that has grown in usage recently is *co-dependency*. Co-dependency is a kind of addiction to a person, relationship, or set of relationships, and the problems and conflicts attached to that person, relationship, or relationships. Thus, an alcoholic, for example, will be connected to a number of co-dependent relationships—persons who have formed and shaped their lives around the alcoholic's addiction. It is estimated that an alcoholic negatively influences around twenty-five to thirty persons. If they do not become fully co-dependent, they are nonetheless negatively influenced by the life-style of the alcoholic. The same pattern happens in most addictive—co-dependent—relationships, whether they are substance or process addictions.

Addictions follow a pattern, whatever the type of addiction may be. A person becomes exceedingly *attached* to someone or something, presumably to derive meaning, belonging, or benefit from the association. The *attachment* builds up a *tolerance*. *Tolerance* refers to the dynamic—"the more I have, the more I want." Addiction is a progressive phenomenon in which a person needs *more* of the substance or process. There is a crucial turning point in the process of addiction: it is the phase of *self-deception*, wherein a person protests that he or she is in control of life, but in fact "is being had," or controlled, by the addicting agent. Other elements included in most addictions are *withdrawal symptoms* when the addictive toxin is not available, and a radical *loss of freedom and meaning*.

In *The Addictive Organization*, Schaef and Fassel discuss how some of the dynamics of addiction can become destructive. Some systems become addictive. Addictive systems are closed systems, not giving its participants many options or choices. Many other characteristics of addicts apply also to organizations and systems: denial of reality, especially of the addiction; confusion; self-preoccupation; dishonesty; pretensions of perfectionism; the illusion of control; preoccupation with a scarcity and the need for more; ethical deterioration. Other addictive signs that can be part of systems are: a crisis orientation, depression, stress, dependency, negativism, defensiveness, tunnel vision, and anxiety.

As with individual addicts, addictive systems need co-dependents to survive. Schaef and Fassel maintain that co-dependents of an addictive system serve in collusion with the system to maintain it. Thus, co-dependents within an addictive system serve as caretakers, volunteers, sufferers, and martyrs. They frequently develop psychosomatic illnesses because of their relationship with the addictive system.

Key to the functioning of addictive systems is control and competition. The addictive organization uses control to get people to do what it wants. The competition inherent in an addictive system is a symptom of the external rather than internal points of reference such organizations use to measure self-worth.

Addictive systems give sick answers to real and important problems. As they persist in the process, the problems compound and become more difficult. Such organizations have a tendency to become ruthless and to lose their brightest and most imaginative and innovative people. For such organizations, there is of necessity an eventual bottoming out.

In short, such systems need recovery. Crucial steps in the recovery process are the rediscovery of a congruence between an organization's mission and its structure, the redevelopment of moral sensitivity, improved and multidirectional communication, the enablement of multilevel leadership, and a renewed sense of innovation. However, whether the addict is an individual or an organization, or whether a person is the co-dependent of an addict or an addictive organization, the basic crucial step is the *admission of powerlessness and how addiction has made life, work, and service unmanageable.*

The Church as Addict

The foregoing discussion of addiction is perhaps another way of getting at the ecclesiological crisis facing the church today. In a real sense, the church has become addicted to what Boff refers to as the traditionalistic vision of Trent and its resulting praxis or style of church. The institutional, hierarchical metaphor or image of church is the one that is still propagated and the one that predominates over many imaginations. Control and order are primary values of the system. Innovation is discouraged. We certainly have had a drain off of bright, creative people. And there are ever more glaring signs that this wobbly organization is coming apart or bottoming out.

Harvey Cox documents well the tension that exists in the church today in his excellent study *The Silencing of Leonardo Boff.* In telling the story of the Vatican's mandating Boff to a period of silence, Cox tells in story-form the violent reactions of an addictive system experiencing the intervention of Boff and other liberation theologians. The Vatican's treatment of Boff is classic in its enfleshment of the addictive theory. A closed system, defensive, determined to give the illusion of control and perfectionism, begins to experience withdrawal symptoms at some of Boff's suggestions about ecclesiology. Boff's admonition that the church move off a *potestas*—worldly power model—to an *exousia*—church grounded in the Spirit of the risen Christ model—annoys, aggravates, and leads to a denial of the real woundedness of the organization, and to a lashing out with guilting techniques and control toward Boff himself, who is simply refusing to be a co-dependent.

Addiction and Grace

Gerald May, Alcoholics Anonymous, and most 12-step programs speak of addictions as misplaced spiritual longings. Each addiction is a misplaced desire for God and for love. The moment of recognition, awareness of powerlessness, is the beginning of a life that confesses the need for God.

The opposite of addiction in May's view is grace. Moving from addiction is a breakdown that becomes a breakthrough to life in the Spirit, under the sway of the love and power of God, the sway of grace.

Applying May's wisdom to the ecclesiological scene, if we are indeed in institutional (addictive) breakdown, the breakthrough, though resisted, is a break through to a church infused and empowered with the Spirit of God, one truly imbued with *exousia,* rather than hiding in the tattered wrappings of *potestas.*

Why Resistance?

Why is there such vehement resistance, from both individuals and systems, to therapeutic movement? Let us consider some of the layers of resistance and their possible causality.

1. A noted expert on international affairs was interviewed recently on a Chicago radio station about the state of relations between nations. When pushed on the question of what is the core issue between the various nations of the world, the expert responded: "It all boils down to *money* and *power.* Nations compete with each other over money and power." I wondered, as I listened, if that is not in part true of the hierarchy's reluctance to look critically at both our dominant ecclesiology and style of church. On the one hand, such a critical look might necessitate a shift in the worldly *potestas* model that dominates ecclesial culture. Secondly, another look at how money is used in the church would also be involved. Can we continue to invest most of the church's funds in seminaries that produce few, questionably qualitative, priests and a school system that is apparently failing to evangelize and catechize well? A critical look might necessitate a change in the hierarchy's notion and use of power and stewardship.

2. How is it that, while the general Catholic population grows in competence and academic credentials, so much of that population remains complacent about current church practice? I frequently say in talks around the Chicago area that most Catholics seem quite content with attending an anonymous, nonparticipative type of liturgy, accompanied by minimal involvement in community. Genuine community, apostolic works, a sense of mission to the world after the eucharistic celebration simply do not seem to be felt needs of the multitude. In a real sense, consumerism has

bled into church life. Individuals and congregations have been placed in a posture of spiritual consumers. This posture is also one of *irresponsibility*—the major responsibility for the work of the reign of God remains with "the professionals." This is not totally a hierarchical aberration. Most Catholics embrace the posture of *irresponsible consumer*. It is safe, non-threatening, and provides a spirituality of comfort devoid of challenge. Obviously, this type of person would resist a change in ecclesiology.

3. Neither the Christian evangelical movement, nor conservative Islamic groups, have the corner on fundamentalism. There is a kind of fundamentalism present in right-wing Roman Catholicism. This fundamentalism accepts current ecclesiology and church discipline without question, largely because it admits of no ambiguity or searching. Leonardo Boff speaks of the *Mater et Magistra*, or mother and teacher, model of church, wherein ecclesial authority has not only all the answers but also decides on what the questions are. There are many within the church who welcome such a "road map, follow the compass" kind of faith. Their eyes are fixed less on the possibility of ushering in the kingdom of God in human history, and more on experiencing the fullness of the kingdom on the other side of death. A life lived in conformity with *Mater et Magistra* dictates insures "a safe place" after death. Again ecclesiological shifts will be resisted in this group too.

4. Finally, let us avoid all finger pointing. *Most* persons who claim to be "of Jesus Christ" are in fact resisting the sway of grace, the power of the Spirit, the demands of the kingdom. Whether members of the hierarchy in the addictive organization, consumer Christians enjoying benign spiritual consumerism and irresponsibility, Catholic fundamentalists or left-of-center writers, thinkers, and believers, who see the toxicity of enforcing "a one-way ecclesiology"—all of us resist the death of transformation in the paschal journey; that is, the life, death, and resurrection process. There is an annihilation of the false self in true conversion, an annihilation that leads to an infusion of grace, Spirit, and power. Even those of us claiming to know and want the revolution of the kingdom fail to completely embrace Jesus' counter-cultural dominant images. We resist allowing ourselves to be grasped fully by the power of the Spirit. Most of us prefer renovation or rearrangement to genuine renewal. I have been struck by the compassion and mercy of nurses and doctors in hospitals, caring for my elderly relatives. I am convinced that I perhaps write and speak more about the reign of God than they do. I am also convinced that they live it, actualize it, more than I do.

Infallibility and Bottoming Out

Jesus' assurance that he will always be with us, the church, the instrument of the kingdom, his promise of the unfailing presence and guidance of the Holy Spirit, is what true *infallibility* is all about. God will never abandon the unfolding kingdom, as served by Christ's church. We in mission will be unfailing; for God's providential love is unfailing. Assured of who we are and the values of our quest, let us hear the challenge. Most addicts and systems, most persons and systems led to a therapeutic process despite resistance, will have a bottoming out. Bottoming out is not so bad. Consider the other alternative in the addiction process—death. The kingdom, God's movement in human history, through the broken vessels of those calling themselves the body of Christ—we have been assured we will not die. Be assured: we have bottomed out often before, and we are bottoming out now. As church we go on half-millennium binges, then spend a few decades bottoming out, to regain some sanity. Then whatever renewal has been accomplished is reified or institutionalized—and we become addicted again.

The bottoming out that the church is experiencing worldwide is frightening, turbulent, and *life-giving*. The bottoming out has included dwindling attendance at services, scarcity of clergy and religious, and the shuttering of many parishes. But the bottoming out has unleashed some things also: the heartfelt conviction that no one ecclesiology can be thrust on local churches; that ecclesiology rises from people and their experiences; the retrieving of the sacraments of initiation and charisms of the Spirit as the true fonts of ministry and service; the rediscovery of household church; the small basic ecclesial community; and the re-imagining of the parish as a network of smaller, interconnected, interdependent cells—to use an overused phrase, "a community of communities." To understand the small community well, we need to turn to the 1950s and Brazil, to catch a glimpse of a church bottoming out, yet being reborn.

5

The Latin American Experience: Basic Ecclesial Communities

A graduate student, in one of the courses I teach on evangelization, reacted strongly several years ago to a presentation that I was making on the kingdom or reign of God. While not disagreeing with most of what I said, he felt there was an important missing element. I had been speaking of the kingdom as the power of God entering human history, the justice of God turning around the injustice of megasystems, a new God-centered vision of life, viewing life with the Abba spirituality of Jesus, a new way of behaving, based on the values of the Rabbi Jesus. The graduate student, someone who had worked in Latin America, did not disagree with most of what I was saying. He felt, however, that I left the kingdom too ethereal, too soft.

"The kingdom is *people*, in a *place*, in a *time, doing and living*, and *transforming* society," he protested. Of course, everything I was saying was mere poetry if not incarnated or enfleshed by real persons in reality. He reminded me of Dr. Thomas Groome's description of the kingdom as "redeemed people" trying to "redeem society." Groome's description of the kingdom is congruent with his whole shared praxis model of religious education. It integrates story-sharing, community, breaking open Scripture, handing on tradition—but then asks the *performative question:* What are we to do based on our sharing? My students are saying that the kingdom or growth in faith expresses itself in behavior, behavior that at least confronts the evil, the demonic, in the world. To understand the birth of small communities in Latin America it is important to keep in mind the basic underpinning that the spiritual is wedded to the political,

30

the real. Faith leads to doing something. Small communities are the cleansing of society, and the church, on the cellular level.

The liberation theologians, like Guillermo Cook, Jon Sobrino, Gustavo Gutiérrez, and Leonardo Boff reflect on the bottoming out and rebirthing that has taken place in Latin America. Brazil is popularly targeted or named as the womb in which Basic Ecclesial Communities were conceived. Though efforts were being made elsewhere, the most powerful, long-lasting spark seems to have been ignited there in the late 1950s. In the 1960s and 70s the flame was fanned further, in that country and other parts of Latin America.

The Brazilian roots of the movement reach back to the 1950s, to an area near Rio de Janeiro, called Barra do Pirai. There, a grassroots, community-based evangelization movement was begun. Central in this movement was Dom Angelo Rossi, who used lay catechists to evangelize regions beyond Barra do Pirai that were not, could not be, reached by pastors. Gradually Angelo began to train laity to do everything possible on a ministerial level. His movement was an attempt to undo the closing of churches and chapels because of the lack of clergy. In the new movement, meeting halls were erected that served as places of prayer, gathering spaces for eucharistic services, schools for religious education, and educational centers for the practical needs of the people.

Use of the radio became an efficient, unifying tool in both catechesis and celebration of the eucharist. By 1963 there were 1,410 centers connected via radio catechesis and also radio celebration of the eucharist with persons participating at the sites of reception. Catechesis became central to each community. The Better World Movement carried renewal through the country. Evangelical teams traveled Brazil. A nationwide pastoral plan, under the guidance of the Brazilian Bishops' Conference, was implemented from 1965 to 1970, with the goal of renewing parishes and other natural gatherings of people for the purpose of generating small base communities. At the famous Medellín Conference small communities were endorsed as the basic means of being and doing church. Then at the Puebla Conference in 1979 small communities were similarly endorsed and promoted. At the conference, Pope John Paul II spoke of God's and the church's *preferential option* for the poor.

Focus on the poor has at least two implications. First of all, if the power of the reign of God is to be found in any of our lives, it will be in our poverty, our limits, our brokenness. The reason why Jesus, and now bishops, choose "the poor" for the advent of God's reign is that the poor, the broken, the limited have the space to allow grace, God's Spirit, to influence their lives. Most human lives are too cluttered, too *attached*, to experience a heartfelt need for God and cooperation with grace. God enters through poverty. Secondly, small communities came together, as we look at the Latin American experience, out of common *need*—that is, the experience of poverty and oppression, and the need for liberation and redemption.

To synthesize, personal conversion is born in poverty. Isolated individuals, in anonymous society, will only bond in communities when they experience their need for "more" (the transcendent) and their need for "help." Communities have been born out of brokenness and poverty in Latin America. The challenge facing the North American church is to help a largely middle-class, comfortable church find and name the subtle poverty present in our own culture and in our way of doing church.

Small Communities: What Do They Do?
How Do They Look?

The persons in small communities and the theologians writing about them do not see small communities as programs or as pieces of the church. Rather they *are* the church, the experience of church. Everything that ought to go on in "the big church," in the sense of parish, goes on also in the small group. Bernard Lee and Michael Cowan's four characteristics of church apply to both the large assembly as well as the small Christian community. Those characteristics are: word *(kerygma)*, worship *(leitourgia)*, life sharing and community *(koinonia)*, and service or ministry *(diakonia)*. (It should be noted that *kerygma* needs to be inclusive of preevangelization, foundational evangelization [acceptance of Jesus as Lord and desire for community] and catechesis.)

Small communities in Brazil, or elsewhere in Latin America, are made up of poor, oppressed people or those concerned about poverty and oppression; who deliberately attend to the sacred Scriptures, the movement of God in life stories and history; who intentionally pray with and for each other; who serve the needs of each other and the world around them. A few words of comment are needed for the last issue.

In North America and Europe, Christians, specifically Catholics, make sharp distinctions between the secular and the sacred, the political and the spiritual. That arrangement is a quite convenient one, for it allows spirituality to never intersect with daily life. In the Latin American base communities, the political (in terms of taking action for the good of society) flows from shared faith and prayer. Political action is "the praxis" that flows from faith. Ministry or service seems to have unfolded in three ages or stages of motivation of the small communities. First the small communities ensured the nurturance ministries of catechesis and sacraments. At another level, they began, as they got to know each other, to genuinely care for each other. Finally, they have begun to confront societal ills and injustices, and take steps to confront them and work for change.

Latest reports speak of small communities operating and taking shape in several ways in Brazil and elsewhere. In urban areas, what were once large parishes have been reconfigured on a geographical miniparish model. The parish remains the parish, but its ministries are largely experienced in the geographical miniparish or segment of the parish. Many services and gatherings are held at miniparish centers. Meetings in homes, in small groups, take place during Lent and Advent, and other devotional times of the year. More emphasis is placed on home meetings in rural parishes, where we find another model. In more rural parishes, members of extended families meet in each others' homes, for adult faith nurturance, catechesis of children, and preparation for sacraments. A third model is a kind of naturally growing parish, based on small communities. In this model, independent small communities, which began in isolation from each other, have gotten to know about each other and attempted some networking. As these various small groups more effectively network, they begin to think of themselves as parish, and even request official recognition as a parish.

Learning from the Latin American Experience

The basic ecclesial communities that were and are being born in Brazil and other parts of Latin America have much to teach the larger church. Small communities are *communion,* the experience of *union with* God and peers. These groups gather to deliberately attend to the spiritual life; but are always focused also on *reality,* and how God is breaking into history through the reality of life. Thus, small communities value the importance of monitoring and improving human relations among the members of the group. Also, the sharing, prayer, and discussion focus on issues like family, neighborhood, the city, the region, the country, the past, the present, the future, culture, history, the economy, politics, and other aspects of *the real*.

Latin American small communities are quick to name the demons that are to be confronted by the communities themselves: selfishness and division. The dawning of the kingdom of God is found in the primal realization that individuals are incomplete without each other. We are made in the image of God, and God is a trinitarian communion. The baptized are called to live as a reflection of that communion.

While small communities in Africa, the Philippines, Europe, and Latin America bear some resemblance to each other in terms of size and structure, each land has put its own unique brand or emphasis on these groups. Latin America's emphasis has been on the marriage between the spiritual and the political. As stated before, small communities have a sense of *total sin,* with both its personal and social dimensions. Small communities in Latin America continue the prophetic work of Jesus, in liberating people and systems from *sin,* for *communion.* In this view, salvation and liberation are synonymous. The dream of liberation is a dream intended not for a few, but for all. A dynamic of action → reflection → prayer → reflected upon action → communion permeates these groups. The dynamic is always focused on the here-and-now situation.

Of special importance in terms of learning is what Latin America is teaching the universal church about ecclesiology. A healthy theology of church can come neither from textbooks or theories, nor be imposed from without. A healthy theology of church or ecclesiology arises from human experience or practice. The Latin American church very much emphasizes a healthy balance among the realities of church, world, and reign of God. The church is the instrument to help realize the new age, vision, and behaviors of the kingdom. Notice that the kingdom is neither relegated to the afterlife nor identified with the church. The kingdom, rather, is unfolding in history. In Latin American ecclesiology the head of the church is the risen Christ, alive in his people, the living body of Christ, and alive and active in people's charisms.

Charisms, charismatic persons, are vital for understanding the Latin American experience. A critique that Boff and others would ascribe to our status quo understandings of ecclesiology and ministry is that we have allowed those who have been ordained to absorb and accumulate all charisms unto themselves. Priests and bishops have become the "dispensers" of all ministries. This, besides being "theological pathology," is also existentially impossible. No mortal person is the deposit of all charisms. A charism is a share in the power of the Holy Spirit, a grace, a gift. A charism is always used in reference back to the divine giver—in praise of God. Charisms also are used for the common good, to help facilitate the dawning of the reign of God in a local community. Gifts used just for self-benefit diminish into mere talents. As mentioned before, in his book *Theology of Ministry*, Thomas O'Meara describes ministry as public activity that flows from baptism. The public activity is the utilization of charisms to help realize the kingdom in a local community. O'Meara's definition of *ministry* in the ideal order is very much the experience of ministry in the Latin American church.

This view of charisms and ministry is revolutionary in that it retrieves the ancient, catechumenal dynamic of church, in which ministry flowed from baptism and the rites of initiation. In this catechumenal model, there was not and is not an accumulation of charisms in a few persons, but rather a sharing in a diversity of charisms and ministries.

Avoiding Congregationalism

In the Latin American church, or indeed any local church, how do groups avoid becoming enclaves, cliques, isolated and atomized little congregations? Though I will treat this issue again, let me address one dimension of it at this point in the study. It is crucial for small groups to see themselves certainly as "the church," but also as contiguous, connected cells of larger bodies: the parish, the local diocesan church, and the church universal. Universality, in the Latin American view, does not mean, however, rigid *uniformity*—another sign of theological pathology. The Latin American church experience encourages universality or catholicity as openness to all that is gospel, and also interpersonal communion or oneness in pursuit of all that is gospel. Such a connotation of *catholic* or *universality* still encourages creativity and diversity of expression.

The Ordained

Bishops, priests, and deacons have important roles in these organisms that are becoming "communities of smaller communities" in Latin America. The ordained are important teachers, animators, and organizers of ministries and communities. Bishops struggle to truly shepherd and prophetically lead their people. Priests are much more than the bishops' clones, in an uncreative, static, systemic uniformity. They are busily engaged in the work of ecclesiogenesis, or the birthing, cleansing, and purifying of the church on the cellular level. Many priests in Latin America, as in an increasing number of places around the world, have to function as itinerants, having several parishes, multiple ministers, and many small communities to animate and serve. Nonetheless, the ordained are important symbols of unity.

The Nonordained and Presiding

The Vatican insistence that the ordinary presider at the eucharist be an ordained, celibate male is a painful situation for the Latin American church. Sunday eucharist in many situations has been replaced by the liturgy of the word and a communion service presided over by a deacon, catechist, or a discerned lay leader. Nonetheless, a eucharistic-type prayerful meal often is held in homes, or at a center, including prayers of praise, a sharing of food and drink, and a commitment to service and ministry. Precision is practiced in language. The word *eucharist* is reserved for the celebration presided over by priest or bishop. In some areas, the words *Lord's Supper* are used for priestless, eucharistic-type services, presided over by the coordinator of the base community. It is commonly accepted that the presence of the risen Christ is real at any such gathering in his name.

Thus, the Latin American church is grappling existentially with what we in parts of North America can still discuss academically—the pastoral crises created by leadership being attached (addicted) to one monolithic, universally imposed way of doing things. Boff and other liberation writers have uncovered writings from the fathers of the church that give evidence of the reality of household churches and the typical practice of the head of the household presiding at the eucharist. Some believe that deaconesses and widows were the leaders of some household churches, thus women probably presided over the blessing and sharing of the sacred bread and cup. The *experience* of church in Brazil and elsewhere is raising pastoral questions that the larger church can no longer afford to avoid: the role of women, the viability of an all-male priesthood, the nature of the presence of Christ at celebrations presided over by the nonordained.

The Institution

I return briefly to the wedding of prayer, reflection, and service or political action in Latin American communities. These communities, grounded in an ecclesiology quite different from the status quo vision of church, have a unique sense of what *power* means. Power is experienced in service, *power* is a share in the glory of the risen Christ. A Latin American critique of status quo, traditionalistic ecclesiological vision and practice is that it is confused with a worldly, pagan sense of power. In fact, some pastoral theologians would say current ecclesial structures are pagan structures that have been blessed with holy water, but remain pagan in their aggressive, controlling understanding of *power*.

The institutional church, vertical in its relationships, worldly/pagan in its power, is devoid of the passion and excitement of the early Christian movement. It is paralyzing, stagnating, sclerotic, and neurotic. Yet the institutional dimension of church is certainly needed. There is always need for pragmatics, organization, coordination, communication, and interconnecting in the movement of the kingdom. Thus, the institution as facilitator of communities is the proper role for the institutional dimension of the church. The critical issue is whether the institution is seen, used, and adapted as tool or servant to God's reign, or whether it is seen as an end in itself. To the degree that it is propagated as an end in itself, to that degree it is idolatrous in nature.

It would be pathology upon pathology to try to use the institution to institutionalize small groups or communities. That would again be an attempt to reify what is a movement of the Holy Spirit. We cannot institutionalize communities. The reality of communities, however, can have a renewing, cleansing effect on the institution. I spoke of this earlier as the renewal or cleansing of the church on the cellular level.

A Pastoral, Practical Interlude

At the Institute of Pastoral Studies where I teach, at parishes where I consult, at conferences I address, I hear the struggle and frustration in many persons who are attempting to ignite the small group movement in the context of a parish fairly well steeped in the institutional motif and traditionalistic ecclesiology. I have been suggesting to such parishes and persons that they consider modest starting points.

We have much to learn from businesses and corporations regarding conviction, passion, and organization in facilitating conversion—both individual and corporate. But I think the institutional model of church took more of a step toward idolatry in adapting too much the trappings of industry. Look at the typical American version of the Vatican II parish. An elite core "on the top" steps forward or is chosen for leadership or ministry. Its members in turn organize themselves in groups called "boards," "councils," or "teams." Church is not business, government, or competitive sports—all of which have boards, councils, and teams. As church we are called to be communion-community.

We would take a small but important step toward renewing the institution if the structures charged with coordination, facilitation, and animation envisioned themselves as *communities*, and acted as such. Remember what we said were the characteristics of community: sharing the word, life, prayer, and service. Boards, councils, and teams often get to the service—or task—without tending to the sharing of word, life, and prayer. Without souls being nourished by sharing word, life, and prayer, ministry quickly becomes tasks, and tasks lead to energy depletion and burnout.

The typical post–Vatican II parish already contains rich potential for movement toward small communities. Let discerning leaders of "cradle-to-grave" religious education ministry re-imagine themselves as the religious education *community*. Let there be similar movements toward a worship *community*, a pastoral care *community*, a youth ministry *community*, a finances and administration *community*. These communities of discerned leaders certainly get to their particular services, based on their charisms, but they would take time also to create a community, by doing communal things with each other. Out of the base of life-giving, renewing community, they would then lead and guide their particular areas of parish life. I also wish that parish governance bodies or parish councils could be re-imagined as parish leadership *communities*. In such a model, discerned leaders of the various ministerial communities, and of the neighborhood pastors (described in a previous chapter), and of the small faith-sharing communities would make up a community that has as its ministry the visioning, dreaming, and planning of the long-range plans for the parish's spiritual renewal and evangelization efforts.

In similar ways, "communal practices" like praying together, sharing stories, sharing Scripture, could be done with typical parish organizations, like men's groups, women's groups, and the like. Some parish organizations become moribund and stagnant as they lose touch with their spiritual roots and origin.

"Adjusting the dials" on already existing parish structures, giving them a "communal spin," could nudge us a bit toward the Latin American experience of small communities—persons gathered around the word, prayer, service, and action.

Base Communities: Principles and Practices

Let us attempt a summary of the experience of small communities in Latin America. A generic description: they regularly meet; they are oppressed believers who gather around the Word, celebrate life and faith, and have the self-concept that they are both signs and instruments of liberation. Above all, the small community is not seen as a technique or program, but rather as the very experience of the dynamics of church.

Groups arise "from the poor." The undergirding theology of small groups is deeply rooted in the paradoxical, counter-cultural vision of the Beatitudes, that somehow God works through and breaks into human history through brokenness, poverty, struggle, vulnerability, hunger, sickness—the underside of life. One dimension of the resistance North American parishes have to the concept of small Christian communities is that they seem to come together and gather around need and poverty. As mentioned in a previous chapter, our individualistic, atomized, anonymous life-styles often blind us to areas of emotional, spiritual, relational poverty in our lives.

Small communities have given rise, in Latin America, to ecclesial structures that are not alienating in nature, structures that facilitate ministry of all the baptized, according to one's giftedness or charism. Such an alive, liberated, "ministering community" model of church stands in stark relief to the consumer church of other parts of the world. In these local churches, baptismal and human rights are violated, and members are not even aware of how they are being violated. On the other hand, the anesthetized consumers could become small communities characterized by multiple, mutual ministries and relationships of responsibility and reciprocity.

Classical theological themes rinse through small communities. Communities believe God is *self-revealing* in the sharing, decisions, and activity of the communities. Two *christological* strains run through the movement.

There is at once a *"low christology,"* a suffering servant christology, which very much emphasizes the Christ of and with the poor. There is simultaneously an emphasis on the *lordship of Christ,* the lordship of the risen Christ—who is most properly seen as the head of the church.

Related to christology is *pneumatology,* or an understanding of the work of the Holy Spirit. The historical, physical Jesus was the enfleshed presence of the Holy Spirit in the world. Now the Holy Spirit in the church is the power and presence of the risen Christ available for us. Thus, in the experience of Latin America small communities, revelation, christology, and pneumatology are inseparably intertwined.

Following the revelation of divine will, under the lordship of the risen Christ, under the sway of the Holy Spirit, small communities transcend self-nurture or maintenance. They see as their responsibility the transformation of society with the power of Jesus and the gospel. These small groups do not inherit history; they shape it, mold it, make it! Stressing a theology of *discipleship*—a small group in close intimacy with the rabbi, Jesus—communities seek to listen for and respond to the counter-cultural call of Christ.

The image of the reign of God and the food of the eucharist are crucial for these small groups. The small communities seek to cooperate with the Spirit in the ushering in of the new age, called God's reign or kingdom. The eucharist, as given to us by Christ, is the *eschatological meal or banquet* that believers share in to both announce and celebrate the new age, and also to help realize its coming.

Though communities take on a myriad of forms and formats in Latin America and around the world, several constants can be found in Latin American base communities: prayer, worship, song, fellowship, intracommunity ministry, and movement outward to pool resources in the transformation of society—especially social evils. Latin American communities embody well Bernard Lee and Michael Cowan's notion of "mystical politicism." It should be noted that it has been the experience of some who have worked in and studied some of the models in parts of Latin America that there is indeed the possibility of misusing the dynamics of small communities for antigospel, political gains—that is, revolutionary purposes—in the worst sense of that term.

6

Glimpses of the African Church

My study of the Latin American movement suggests to me that initially small communities were spontaneous grassroots experiences. The Medillín and Puebla conferences (among others) and the Better World Movement have gone on to "institutionalize" them as the normative way to do church. Perhaps building on the Latin American experiment and success, the African hierarchy was quick to see in small Christian communities an effective means to be and do church—especially in areas where clergy are few in number.

Much of what I will say in this chapter is an analysis of the work of Fritz Lobinger and his staff of the Lumko Missiological Institute, in southeast Africa. In fact, all of East Africa represents the part of the continent where the highest concentration of small communities exists, because almost fifteen years ago the episcopal conference established small communities as the ideal for parish renewal and the propagation of faith. They exist in other parts of Africa as well. African small communities seem more conservative and less highly politicized than their parallels in Latin America. They are essentially a way of keeping church alive, though Lobinger and others are devising strategies for transforming the communities into more politically aware and active organisms.

I focus on St. Simon's parish, a parish of about one thousand Catholics, a Xhosa community, near the Indian Ocean. The parish has been in existence for over fifty years. Fritz Lobinger, several years ago, began to help out there on occasion, presiding at occasional Sunday liturgies. On the other Sundays and other days of the week, the parish was pastored by a catechist, who was employed full-time to care for all daily pastoral needs. As with many parishes in Africa, Lobinger found St. Simon's to be a colonialized African community living out a West European style of

41

parish. He found the community to be, in his words, a community of spiritual "consumers." Despite the fact that the community was pastored by a catechist, it had allowed that catechist to absorb all ministerial roles, or pretend that he had all charisms needed for ministry. The people had relinquished all ministerial responsibility, indeed never had an awakening that ministry was both their right and responsibility. The dominion of the catechist over parish responsibilities terminated with an accident that left the catechist severely debilitated. This *total dependence period* of the community on the catechist ended; the community entered another phase, a phase of confusion. A person came forward to take the catechist's place. The catechist had allowed no one but himself to read at Sunday gatherings. This new person came forward to assume the lectoring role. He quickly grew bored with the responsibility and began to be irregular in showing up on Sundays. When eucharist was to occur, this left the ministry of proclaiming the first readings to the priest. With insight, Lobinger refused. He simply went on to do his appropriate ministry, the proclamation of the gospel.

Notice the dynamics so far: first a catechist, then another man, ran the community with a nouveau-clerical, vertical ecclesiology. The other man replacing the catechist was not the result of any communal discernment, or group consensus. Rather he usurped control. Operating out of an impoverished motivation at best, he dropped activity when it no longer pleased him. The priest in turn refused to "do for." He left a gaping hole in the liturgy of the word so that behaviorally he might teach the community, move its members, to a renewed ecclesial consciousness.

A new phase of St. Simon's growth began with the priest asking one Sunday how parishioners felt about omitting the first readings. When they generally communicated a disappointment in what was happening, he asked whether some persons could come forward to be trained and commissioned for lectoring. Almost thirty people, including women, came forward. They constituted the first ministerial team that engaged in systematic training with the visiting priest. Soon other ministering groups emerged, and then a parish council to bring order to the ministries. Ministers were always liturgically commissioned or installed, so as to more and more imbue the community with an attitude of ministerial responsibility. Surrounding parishes, in an attempt to break from their "consumer church" style, began to send people to St. Simon for ministerial training.

A great advance happened when the people themselves came up with the idea of small neighborhood groups. The idea of small communities was explained to the whole congregation. The neighborhood seemed to provide the natural web or foundation for the communities, five of which began. The communities gathered around the catechesis of their children, and also small group ministering to neighbors in need. Both of these ministries required the priest taking on the role of training and enablement. The small communities, Lobinger reports, lasted only six months.

With great wisdom, however, the parish did not throw in the towel on small communities. Rather, they reinstituted them, in fact starting a few more. This time, however, they built in regular interaction among the groups, exchanging ideas, formats, etc.; and they reconfigured the parish council to include crucial representation from the small groups. We can see here an important learning. Small groups cannot just be overlayed on everything else done in a parish. Small groups cannot be institutionalized, but parish structure needs to be reshaped to support and nurture small groups and to reflect that small groups are a filter or prism through which parish is experienced. At this stage, Lobinger began to feel that St. Simon's was becoming what he calls a community of communities.

At the present moment, St. Simon's finds itself grappling with three issues. First of all, the communities are trying to deal with larger issues of social justice ministry, or to influence the institutions and systems around them that seem to contribute to peoples' plight and pain. Secondly, St. Simon's is trying to not fall into the dark hole of parochial narcissism. Thus, it is trying to remind itself of its connectedness to other parishes and the universal church. Finally, in an ongoing way, St. Simon's is confronting the chronic problem of "community vs. domination." Even in this rich pastoral experiment, "lay clericalism, vertical ecclesiology" became an issue, with some ministers in effect dominating others, becoming a kind of ministerial elite. A little bit later in this chapter, I will explore their creative way of confronting these issues.

Look . . . Listen . . . Love

St. Simon's has become a kind of teaching parish for neighboring parishes. It has served as a laboratory for Lobinger's Lumko Institute, which produces training materials that now are used in many parts of Africa. The St. Simon's-Lumko discipline for small groups has been kept deliberately simple, to minister to and help the simple folk of African villages. The value of their discipline is that it is indeed an interior discipline on how to do and be in small groups. The strategy or discipline is not a program. Programs are terminal in nature; they end. They are a *product*, often produced by people who are not familiar with the myriad of cultures in which Christian communities are founded.

Father Vincent Donovan discovered this cultural issue, one that often creates a blockage in the generation of communities, in his work in Africa. Donovan writes beautifully in his classic *Christianity Rediscovered* that true missionary work must not just be the colonialization of the Western world's version of Catholicism or Christianity vis-à-vis Third World nations. Rather the core values and realities of the kingdom must emerge from the unique culture of every people and land. Relative to our analysis of the small group movement, small groups will be successful in those efforts that are respectful of culture, and which teach a simple, human discipline of being a community rather than imposing a program.

Small groups in St. Simon's are made up of neighbors or extended family members. In St. Simon's and other communities using Lumko Institute strategies, three steps are taken in each community meeting:

1. *Look at life.* In this stage, participants share stories of the happenings of their lives, their neighborhood, their world since the small group has last met.

2. *Listen to life.* Participants are encouraged to sit in silence for a short period of time to reflect on how God may be speaking to them through the collective stories of the group. In a second part of the listen stage, Scripture is proclaimed—either from the lectionary or other passages that group leaders judge appropriate. Again silence ensues, with the follow-up question of how God is speaking now through the scriptural word.

3. *Love.* As the meeting closes, the community, as community and individuals, ask concretely how they can put into behavior the Christian commandment to love. This concretization of love may include personal efforts in the family, among friends, at work, in the neighborhood. It may also include individual group attempts at bringing the gospel to confront/critique injustice in the neighborhood, or some institution or system that has impact on the small group's life.

The look-listen-love methodology is an interior discipline that group members appropriate. It is not a program, but dispositions, attitudes, and skills that people can use in community with any sort of catechetical materials, perhaps just the lectionary or Scripture. The three steps are adapted by the Lumko Institute for other efforts. There are *Awareness* programs, which use the three steps of community sharing to help participants grow in awareness and understanding of some issue important to their lives, like growth in marriage or parenting. The steps are also used in *Amos* programs, named after the prophet. Amos programs guide the small communities toward some prophetic action regarding societal, institutional, or systematic injustice or evils.

Volunteerism vs. Baptismal Spirituality and Ministry

A crisis developed at St. Simon's, as it does at any parish seriously dealing with what is popularly called "lay ministry." As more and more people became interested, not only in small communities but in various ministries either to a small group or the larger church, a kind of clericalism emerged among the laity. It seemed the natural thing to do, to slip into a hierarchical, power-oriented model of church. People began to use ministry, and leadership in ministry, to make their importance felt. Some faithful, feeling this tone emerging, brought the issue to a council meeting. They interceded with those present that St. Simon's, and the other parishes following their plan, had a responsibility to the larger church—that is, to model a different way of being church. Their counter-cultural and counter-ecclesial culture contribution had to be a faith community where the modus operandi of world and church—a power model—was not used.

St. Simon's, and now the Lumko Institute, which propagates renewal efforts around Africa, speaks of "emerging leaders," rather than volunteers, in describing people acting on their baptismal right and responsibility to minister. To eradicate elitism or a vertical ecclesiology in so-called "lay ministry," several therapeutic steps were taken. First, much of the ministry was placed in the hands of the small groups. Rather than alienating structures that had people ministering all over the geographical parish, people are encouraged to use their gifts to benefit their own natural community. In addition, relative to the needs of the small community, one person is never raised up and trained for a given ministry; several persons are trained for several ministries. This eliminates the human tendency to rank individuals in order of importance or control. A third therapeutic intervention has been to insure that whether persons are ministering to a small group or the larger parish, they belong to an additional community, a ministering community—in which they are trained, in which also they receive ongoing formation, support, and nurturance. All ministry comes from and is directed back to the community.

Ministerial training is a spiritual activity in these African communities. Ministerial training is looked on as the unleashing of the power of the Holy Spirit, enfleshed in the gifts and charisms of each of the baptized. Real effort is given to not use the seminary metaphor in the ministerial training of the baptized. As much as possible, each local parish is encouraged to do its own training, play down the aura of "sending people to special places for special training." Parishioners come to centers to hear a special speaker who cannot get to every parish community, or to experience some training that is important for all to have. In addition, rather than heavy cerebral content, the content of ministerial training focuses largely on skills training, then on theological reflection. "Skills training—theological reflection—doing" is the methodology that is largely employed.

The commissioning of ministers is something that not only the African church, but also the American church, has begun to face. The public nature of ministry cries out for rituals that express discernment of charisms, election or choice by the community, and the commissioning or charging by the community. Here also careful consideration needs to be given to ecclesiology; for ecclesiology—implicit or explicit—always flows into and expresses itself in ritual. The commissioning of ministers, whether in Africa or America, ought not to speak of an ordination to an ontologically different state of being, or a setting apart from the community. Commissioning rituals ought to ritualize a deep immersion into the community and the marketplace, the world.

The Better World Movement

Another force, besides the Lumko Institute, in fostering pastoral renewal and small community development in Africa (as well as other Third World countries) has been the Better World Movement. Beginning with base communities in Latin America and moving to Africa and elsewhere, the Better World Movement has developed a flexible map of what a parish could and should look like. I stress the word *flexible*, for this mapping is

Figure 1: Zone Coordination Teams

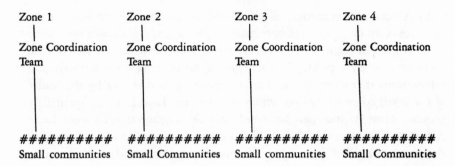

Zone 1	Zone 2	Zone 3	Zone 4
Zone Coordination Team	Zone Coordination Team	Zone Coordination Team	Zone Coordination Team
##########	##########	##########	##########
Small communities	Small Communities	Small communities	Small Communities

but a guide in visioning parish. Key to understanding the Better World vision is the concept of *zoning.* Each parish is divided into zones. A kind of "middle-management" ministerial community coordinates tne ministries and faith life of each zone. Each such community is called a *zone coordination team.* A parish design or structure would include four ministerial bodies: a *pastoral council,* which does long-range planning; a *pastoral ministry* commission, which implements plans of the pastoral council; a *community of ministers,* those engaged in ministry in the parish; and a *community of priests and religious,* the ordained or professed who serve as itinerants, both interparish and intraparish. Each zone has its own zone coordination team, whose members minister to the small communities. See Figure 1.

In this vision or mapping, the itinerant priest passing from zone to zone, or small community to small community, is the symbol of unity and universality. The deacon or lay catechist often serves as the pastoring, shepherding figure. The zone coordination teams provide training for and also direct ministry to the many small communities that comprise a zone; these zone teams are composed of people from the community of ministers. Each small community contains up to twenty units, households or families.

"Dry Mass" vs. Eucharist

In African communities, as elsewhere, eucharist is dependent on the presence of an ordained, celibate male. I have already discussed how some Latin American communities reserve the title *eucharist* for the sacred meal presided over by a priest, but also are experimenting with home-bound celebrations that they call the Lord's Supper—presided over by the leader of the small community—at which they feel the Lord is really, spiritually present. Most African parishes would not be as progressive as some Latin American communities. The Sabbath experience tends to be a liturgy of the word, presided over by a deacon or catechist, and a communion service, using ministers of the eucharist. Such is the practice also in the Phillippines, where this communion service is frequently referred to as a "dry Mass."

One can intuit the inherent confusion in the minds of simple, ordinary people when they experience eucharistic-type services that are not eucharists; eucharist-type home gatherings that are not eucharists; a priest present in assembly, and then not present. Without quality catechesis, people would have a tendency to lump together all such rituals as Mass or eucharist. Their benign ignorance is not as worrisome as the malevolent addictive leadership and structures that would deprive communities of the eucharist.

"Emergent" as a Key Perspective

I mentioned earlier that Fritz Lobinger and others in the Lumko Institute stress the image of the *emerging* leader. The image suggests that something is developing organically, naturally in the body of Christ. Leaders and ministers—nonordained—are emerging. The emergence of small communities and leaders-ministers indeed appears to be a movement of the Holy Spirit. One of my students at Chicago's Loyola Institute for Pastoral Studies speaks of the so-called priest-shortage as "God cleaning house," getting us back to where we should be.

In his excellent study *The Emerging Pastor: Non-ordained Catholic Pastors,* Peter Gilmour says another phenomenon is occurring globally—nonordained men and women who are pastoring parishes. Gilmour says there are four possible perspectives from which to view and interpret this phenomenon. The *substitution* perspective suggests that these nonordained persons are filling in for the normative male, celibate, ordained, who will return in ample supply. The *management perspective* is a realistic perspective in which an ordinary and diocese look at the needs and try to provide "coverage" as best they can. The *ministry perspective* says all of God's people can and should minister/pastor in different ways because of baptism. The *community* perspective, flowing from the previous perspective, says that communities will always reconfigure themselves to provide the leadership and pastoring needed for a given time. Gilmour suggests that some of what this book is about has been going on—unheralded—for years, decades, in parts of the United States that are "priestless."

7

Models of Communities—
North American and Evangelical

Two names well known in Protestant evangelical circles are those of Dr. Paul Cho and Dr. John Hurston. Cho and Hurston worked together in Seoul, South Korea, in the building of the Full Gospel Yoido Church. Literally hundreds of thousands claim membership in this church, most of whom are part of small groups. The Cho-Hurston model of generating small groups has been transported to America and used by evangelical churches, among them the Assembly of God.

The Cho-Hurston vision of church as a network of small home cell units is anchored specifically in two passages of Scripture: Joel 2:13–27 and Acts 2:4. The Joel passage reminds us that God is acting in human history, calling each to repentance. God wills the restitution and restoration of the human family. God is alive among human beings, restoring, saving. The fulfillment of God's Old Testament promise and hope of restoration is found in Acts 2. It is the story of the birthing of the church. Whether one is attracted to Cho-Hurston strategies or not, the dynamics of Acts 2 are vital for anyone interested in evangelization and small groups.

Luke tells us that the beginning of the church is a movement of the Holy Spirit, a movement that prompted Peter to evangelize. Peter's evangelization set his listeners' hearts astir, into an inner search. "What are we to do?" they ask. Peter responds with an admonition to reform, reform that will express itself in the ritual of baptism. Thousands were added that day. Those who were converted certainly kept attending worship at the large church, the temple. But we are told that they also met in their homes for the breaking of the bread and prayer. Social justice was not an

50

afterthought or appendage. Rather they truly lived the communal life, dividing up their property, based on each other's needs. Daily numbers were added to their gathering.

The early Christian movement simply continued the tradition begun in Judaism of joining temple to "household church." The Joel-Acts convergence says to us: God's saving work continues, flows through the shared lives and faith of household churches and small communities. Beginning in Korea, extending now into North America, the Cho-Hurston vision is rooted in a scriptural conviction that God wills renewal through communion, community.

A significant contribution from Drs. Cho and Hurston to the evangelical movement toward small communities is their notion of building communities on persons' natural webs or weavings of relationships. Rather than try to impose group structures on people, Cho and Hurston found the more effective strategy to be to form groups around common needs, friendship groups, family ties, people with common interests, people who share a common ministry. Those whose mission it is to facilitate small groups do well to breathe life into already existent groups or those waiting, in embryo, to become community. In other words, a parish staff ought not to impose foreign, strange groupings onto people.

A Pragmatic, Functional Hierarchy

In many evangelical churches influenced by Cho and Hurston's pioneering efforts, one of the full-time staff members would be a pastor or coordinator—or head—of small communities. The leader of small communities is assisted by a general secretary, who serves as an important intermediary between pastor, the coordinator of small communities, and the middle-management team of district heads and section leaders. The district heads and section leaders are not to be viewed in geographical terms. Rather, district heads and section leaders represent leadership based on natural webbings and weavings. District heads work with the pastor, the coordinator of small communities, and the general secretary in designing material of a catechetical nature to be used in the small groups. District heads in turn pass this material on to section leaders. Section leaders are "carrier teachers" who bring the material to the leaders of the small communities, or the small cell leaders. The model is diagramed in Figure 2.

Figure 2: The Cho-Hurston Model of Church

the pastor and pastoral staff → work with the coordinator of small communities; the general secretary is an important intermediary between middle management, the small groups, the coordinator, and pastor and pastoral staff

district heads work with the staff and coordinator in generating materials for the small groups

they train section leaders, carrier teachers, who train the leaders of small cell groups to implement the material in their small group of about fifteen adults, couples, or family units.

Through the ministry of the general secretary there is always a flow of feedback and communication, from the smallest organism, the small cell group, to and from the pastor and coordinator. The similarity between the Better World praxis and the evangelical model is obvious.

Different Tones/Emphases for Different Groups

In different circles of evangelical Christianity, we find different groups taking on different packaging, shapes, and sizes. For example, there are:

1. Bible study groups that make their primary function the study of Scripture
2. prayer groups that gather largely for prayer
3. fellowship groups that gather largely for friendship and shared social experiences
4. task groups that take on a common project or ministry
5. accountability groups that focus on discipleship, study, and confrontation of problematic areas of life

6. covenant groups that take on the functions of the first five groups but are open to a rotating variety of ministries (their prime function is to grow in discipleship and ministry)
7. house church groups that perform actual church services at someone's home

Drs. Cho and Hurston have discovered further that the ideal small group size is fifteen units or families.

Let us splice together two ideas then: small groups seem to proliferate in evangelical Christianity when the animator/facilitator/coordinator helps potential candidates find a natural weaving or webbing, or set of relationships; and the type of group that best serves their healthy self-interest. Something that I will touch on later when I explore adult faith formation is that adults are pragmatic and practical, willing to participate in things that help them live better lives.

A Covenant Group

Let us look at one model from the many that Dr. Hurston teaches in Dallas, Texas: the Covenant Group. The format of a typical Covenant Group is as follows:

7:00 to 7:15	Arrival and informal socializing
7:15 to 7:30	Worship in song
7:30 to 8:00	Group leader facilitates teaching component, comprised of Scripture reading and prepared discussion questions
8:00 to 8:30	One-on-one ministering through shared prayer and conversation, done in units of two
8:30 to 9:00	Social time—to nurture relationships

In this model the 7:30 to 8:00 teaching has a rotating thematic agenda, called the seven pillars of growth. The group focuses on one each week following a full seven-week cycle, beginning the cycle over again at the end of seven weeks. This "seven pillars notion" is borrowed from Proverbs 9: "Wisdom has built herself a house; she has erected her seven pillars." Those seven pillars, or rotating themes are:

1. God and Spirit
2. health and body

3. mind or soul
4. family and relationships
5. career or business
6. finances
7. ministry and service

Principles Behind Small Cell Groups

Dr. Cho, Dr. Hurston, and other evangelical leaders animate and generate small groups based on principles or convictions. Among them are the following:

1. People's lives are enriched and nurtured in small groups; every individual could profit from the spiritual intimacy of a small group.

2. Ministries are more effective, caring, and informal on the small cell group level.

3. In small groups, prayer can be geared to the specific needs of participants.

4. Homes can be transformed into places of systematic Bible study. Scripture can be prayed over and studied pastorally and practically rather than academically.

5. Especially if they are inclusive and inviting, these groups can become effective tools for evangelization.

6. Such groups become dwelling places of the Holy Spirit and environments where baptism in the Holy Spirit can take place.

7. People will gravitate to different types of groups, based on needs and life situations.

Whatever type of group a given gathering of people might evolve into, all such groups in the evangelical context, function to:

1. nurture the faith life of each of the members
2. engage in communal worship around God's word
3. give an experience of real community, or shared life and faith
4. engage in some sort of mission and ministry to others

Small-Group Leadership Discernment

In the Cho-Hurston and other evangelical models of small groups, how are leaders recruited? The pastor, staff, deacons, deaconesses, and elders (and other possible staff leadership persons) look for the following characteristics:

1. a person who seems to be struggling to do God's will and listening to God's call
2. prayerfulness
3. heartfelt faith
4. compassion
5. ability to communicate
6. teachableness
7. willingness to prepare and study
8. ability to inspire, motivate, and unite others

Dr. Hurston explained to me recently that community leaders are trained according to the "Jesus style" of training. When Jesus trained his leaders—disciples and apostles—he, in effect, said, "Listen to My words. . . .Watch Me. . . .I send you out. . . .Come and report back. . . ." The four movements of training are: formal teaching; being in a model group; leading or serving as an assistant leader in an actual group; and a regular experience of supervision. The training of small group leaders is, then, both preparatory and ongoing.

Diverse Ministries

Much like the Roman Catholic experience of the RCIA small-group experience, in an evangelically based small group, there are diverse ministers and ministries. Gifts and charisms need to be discerned.

There is the leader or leaders, responsible for guidance, facilitating shared wisdom, scheduling, location setting, getting to know group members well, and pastoring the group.

There could be also an assistant leader, who often is engaged in on-the-job training.

There is the ministry of the host or hostess, who provides refreshments and other forms of hospitality.

The worship leader calls to and leads in prayer.

The prayer coordinator keeps in touch with the intentions and needs of members and others, and networks this information to the group.

The children's leader goes to an alternate part of the home, to do group work with children, so as to make the experience a more totally family experience.

The outreach minister does proactive outreach to potential new members.

Several of these, and other potential roles, may be carried out by one or more persons on a rotating basis.

Continuation of Groups: Basic Principles

Though now a senior citizen, Dr. Hurston vigorously pursues his commitment to small groups and the cell as the basic unit of church. His most recent work has been at the Word of Faith Outreach Center in Dallas, Texas. Teaching recently, Dr. Hurston reflected on the following convictions. Hurston believes that small groups or cells are organisms, not organizations. Organisms are constantly mutating, changing entities. To best minister to these constantly shifting organisms, there must be a *focused* ministry to leadership of the small cells. As mentioned earlier, the Cho-Hurston model calls for ongoing group leader supervision, which is, in effect, ongoing training. Hurston also refers to the informal, spontaneous times when leaders go to other leaders, or pastoral staff members, for guidance, advice, and leadership.

A pastor will quickly burn out if all small group resourcing is up to *the one* pastoral figure. It is important for a community, seeking to become a community of communities, to be served by a pastoral staff that shares in the pastor's conviction about the importance of small communities. In such a situation, the entire staff can serve as resources to division or section leaders, and specifically, the leaders of each small group.

Dr. Hurston agrees with a Catholic visionary in the small-group movement, J. Gordon Myers, that ongoing evaluation of the small group's progress, or mood, is of vital importance. Myers stresses the importance of the group leader in a recurrent way, raising the question of "How are we doing relative to our vision and goals?" Hurston speaks of the need of "making course corrections." I used another metaphor in a book on evangelization in referring to *shaping*. Shaping is an alternative to throwing in the towel when there is apparent failure. Rather than wasting energy lamenting what did not work well, *shaping* is a process that remains committed to the original vision, but is open and honest enough to reshape, refashion, the modus operandi of a group to better meet its needs now. *Shaping* does not get stuck in the language of failure. It seeks rather to fix what is not working well.

Hurston continues to stress ongoing education about and calling to small-group living from the pulpit. A steady, continuous flow of information about and motivation for small groups would seem to be more of a need in the Catholic Church, where, as discussed earlier, our ecclesiology and consequent pastoral practice seem to have precluded the need for such things as small groups. It takes time to turn around a big ship, unlike the turning around of a small ship. Thus, discouragement is to be expected as part of the process in generating small groups. Group dynamics, to be discussed more in detail later, are vital in the training and nurturance of small-group leaders.

Dr. Paul Yonggi Cho, from whom Tilton and Hurston have learned much, also has strong convictions about small groups. Chief among his convictions are on the centrality of the *pastor* for small groups to work. Cho says that it is the pastor who is *the key player* in a parish becoming a community of communities. We will see later that author, pastor, teacher, Fr. Art Baranowski, has come to the same conclusion himself after over ten years of small-group work in Roman Catholic circles. A parish as a network of small groups is a system, and every system needs a central point. In this case, it is the pastor. The pastor must motivate the congregation; the pastor must put total energy into such a reconfiguration of church life. Home pastors, or cell leaders, need to feel that they are among the pastor's top priorities, and have also some sort of regular access to him.

Cho has moved from a free-flowing kind of small-group experience to one that is intimately related to upcoming large church gatherings—our equivalent to weekend eucharist. Group leaders are made aware of upcoming readings and sermon outlines, and are instructed/trained in their use at the small cell meeting. Cho believes that to the degree that the pastor or a pastoral staff person cannot be personally present to train small-group leaders, staff members should at least use the tools of the age, and communicate with cell leaders via audio or video cassette. In Cho's groups, several elements are constant: singing, prepared teaching, one-on-one ministering, Scripture sharing, group discussion, prayer—which can be intercessory, praise-filled, repentent, or healing in nature; and *evangelization*. Evangelization means that the groups exist to help people increasingly get closer to the Lord. Also, each member is encouraged to consciously try to bring unchurched or unconverted people to the group meetings. Cho believes effective meetings need last only sixty minutes.

Reference was made earlier to a certain hierarchy, or pragmatic flow chart, in the Cho-Hurston vision. Recognizing the principle of natural weavings or webbings, district leaders are responsible for section leaders. Section leaders are responsible for home cell leaders. The district leaders are directly responsible *to* the pastor, the coordinator of small groups, and the general secretary.

The NET

Briefly let us consider John and Karen Hurston's (Dr. Hurston's daughter) original metaphor of the *net* or the *web* for effective evangelization. Every thread in a home-based small group is a relationship; the cluster of relationships constitutes a *net*. The net of small groups is made up of both vertical and horizontal relationships. The vertical ones often are leadership-type ones. But of even more importance are the horizontal ones, the peer-to-peer ones, that constitute horizontal ministries. The pastor, the small-group leader—anyone in leadership in the small community system, must become sensitive to the presence of *holes,* in fact the inevitability of holes, in the nets of small groups. It is essential to grow in the ability to both discern the signs of and to mend those holes. For, indeed, the *net* of the group is the tool by which church members are both gained and lost.

8

Small Groups and Justice

Michael Cowan and Bernard Lee, in *Dangerous Memories,* reiterate a key insight from Paul VI's encyclical on evangelization. Throughout the encyclical there are implicit warnings to not oversimplify or overprivatize evangelization. Specifically, the key insight that Cowan and Lee reiterate, and then connect with the phenomenon of small communities, is the intimate connection between evangelization and social justice. For Paul VI to speak of evangelization without an awareness of how preaching and living the gospel are related is to indeed have a weak, anemic understanding of a richly nuanced, highly connotated term. Cowan and Lee are perhaps more poetic in their magnification of Paul VI's understanding. They speak of small groups as gatherings of persons, in faith, to engage in "mystical politicism," or prayerful, faithful reflection on and action directed toward reality.

We return, then, to the highly politicized nature of Latin American small communities. In a previous chapter, we discussed how these small groups do not dichotomize between the real and the spiritual. Rather, the power of the Spirit, and the charisms of individuals in the small groups, point out and prompt the group outward toward social change, a confrontation with the injustices present in reality. Small groups are often founded in poverty. In poverty the group finds God breaking into history; in poverty individuals and groups are called to missionary social change activity. Cowan and Lee, in trying to adopt this vision for other parts of the globe, describe small communities as experiences of "mystical politicism," from which believers move to "evangelize the megasystems" of society. The megasystems include the areas of economics, politics, religion, and all other institutions that have a tendency to reify and self-perpetuate themselves.

Many Christians tend to compartmentalize things: some do evangelization in the parish, while others do works of justice. The challenge
according to Paul VI, Lee and Cowan, and others doing research in this
area, is to break down needless walls of compartmentalization. Can small
groups be involved in both evangelization and social justice? One evangelical church in Washington, D.C., has discovered that it can.

Rev. Gordon Cosby has been the animating force behind the Church of
Our Savior, in the national capital. Cosby teaches his congregation that
Christians grow in vision—a sense of mission, and passion—only in
relationships, in small groups. It is important, in Cosby's view, to high-
light the reality of *passion*. Passion, he feels, is the missing ingredient in
many parishes and Christian communities. The absence of passion in a
faith community speaks of a lack of direction, purpose, or will power—or
of those energies being misdirected in a faith community. To arrive at
vision, mission, and passion, a small faith group—of not more than three
to thirteen members must consciously listen and attend to the unique call
of Jesus to the group.

The call of Christ to a group (and the individuals therein) is always
threefold:

1. *The call to leave the culture.* Cosby feels we need to be brutally honest
with ourselves about the nature of American culture. It is becoming
increasingly idolatrous, agnostic, or atheistic in nature. We are living, in
fact, in a kind of post-Christian era. The Church of Our Savior community
sees many Americans as addicted to this Godless culture. Much like a
recovering addict, we need to declare our spiritual bankruptcy, or powerlessness, over some of the forces of the culture, and surrender to the
healing power of Jesus, and the love of the small group.

2. *The call to become who we are meant to be.* Who are we meant to be?
Cosby says we are to become "the icons of Christ." When others observe
believers they should see Jesus incarnated again in flesh; they ought to see
the mercy, compassion, justice, and love of Christ.

3. *The naming of a group's counter-cultural mission.* As a small Christian
community intentionally leaves the culture, and struggles to become the
icon of Christ, the group becomes increasingly aware of the woundedness
of society: the millions in this country in poverty and hunger, the huge
number in prisons (there are more persons in prison in America than in
any other country), and other social issues. Step by step a small group
discerns and then decides on a counter-cultural mission and ministry to
some subpopulation that is a victim of society's injustices.

In Addition . . . Maintenance Ministries

For the Church of Our Savior to continue functioning, there must also be maintenance ministries (like lectoring, teaching children, etc.). Small-community members engage, then, in two types of ministry—that which is small-group based and focused on the world, and that which is focused on the ongoing life of the larger church. To belong to the Church of Our Savior is a challenging investment of time and energy. It requires:

1. up to two years of educational preparation to be in a small mission group
2. involvement in a regularly meeting small faith or mission group
3. the counter-cultural mission and ministry of the group
4. possible maintenance ministries
5. weekly worship
6. forty-five minutes of individual prayer and Scripture study daily

Too Much Maintenance, Not Enough Mission

In some of the best Catholic parishes in the country, there may be many ministries and programs operative, but most are maintenance in nature. Few have the tone of "counter-cultural mission" that Cosby's groups do. The Church of Our Savior is a community of missionary, counter-cultural communities. Even those Catholic parishes that have small groups fail, often, in the reach-out missionary component. It is easy for small groups to become self-focused. Actually, there is a danger for small groups to become reductionistic in either of two directions. Some take on a "retreat from the world," otherworldly orientation. Others can become too much "activity" or "mission" oriented. Cosby's church strikes a balance. Quality time is given to what Thomas Merton called "the journey inward" and "the journey outward."

The Church of Our Savior stands as a challenge to Catholic and Protestant parishes alike. Well-known small community and social justice advocate Jim Wallis, writing in his classic *The Call to Conversion*, says that too many of us carve out for ourselves a comfortable Christianity, one that is "spiritually lukewarm" and "politically conforming." In this apathy or lethargy we, in effect, "betray the power of the gospel." We bend the gospel to fit us, rather than allow the gospel to *both* comfort and challenge us.

While many persons enter into small groups for "something more," that something more must transcend the feelings of belonging or the spiritual nurturance that a small group offers. To be true to the call of Jesus, "the more" of a group must include an orientation to the world and its woundedness. The Lord judges us not according to our liturgical styles, nor according to our doctrinal conformity with the magisterium. We are judged, according to the Scriptures, on our compassion.

Cosby's adaptation of small groups for the Washington scene is evocative of the politicized communities of Latin America and Lumko's African "Amos programs." He gives a worldly connotation to the *diakonia*, or service, ministry that must be a part of every small community. Cosby's model, like the parallel Sojouners community and movement, is "world friendly," rather than a retreat from the world. The practical justice emphasis of some small communities mirrors a truth about adults that I will dwell on later: that, relative to education and formation, adults are practical learners. Adults do not want to attend functions that make them store information for the future. Rather they want to be part of experiences that help them live, experiences that improve life in some way.

9
Models—North American and Roman Catholic

In no way can this chapter adequately explain or do justice to the fine pastoral work being done by many here in North America in small communities. In fact, some who are mentioned in this chapter have themselves published. While I try to summarize the broad strokes of their work, their own books—specifically the work of Art Baranowski and Thomas Maney—can flesh out to a great degree the detail their efforts have taken them into. We will look at five models of small communities successful in Roman Catholic contexts: what is termed OIKOS evangelism at St. Boniface's parish, Pembrooke Pines, Florida; the three-stage evolution of small communities at St. Elizabeth Seton's in the archdiocese of Detroit; the Neighborhood Mission process initiated by Father Thomas Maney and others in the Duluth area (and now spread elsewhere); the excellent Scripture study/small group process out of the diocese of Little Rock, popularly known as Little Rock Scripture Study; and the parish spirituality process piloted by the Office for Chicago Catholic Evangelization in the archdiocese of Chicago.

1. Evangelizing through the *Oikos*

Father Michael Eivers, Deacon A. Perry Vitale, and others on the staff of St. Boniface's in the archdiocese of Miami have studied the works of Drs. Cho and Hurston in Seoul, South Korea, and Dr. Hurston's continuing work with his daughter, Karen, and Rev. Robert Tilton. They have taken the basic model discussed in a previous chapter and put it to work in a typical, suburban parish.

Key to understanding the Eivers model is understanding the concept of the *oikos*. *Oikos* is the Greek word for household. Eivers and his staff have extended the notion of household to include the following:

1. kinship: those who make up one's family ties
2. location: those living in geographical proximity
3. interests: those who have common interests or hobbies
4. vocation: those with whom one interacts regularly through job

Father Eivers believes and teaches that the most natural way to evangelize is through the natural ties that comprise each person's *oikos*. Personal invitation and interpersonal relating via the *oikos* is also the natural way to lead people into small communities. At St. Boniface's, evangelistic outreach is intimately connected with awakening persons to an attitude of outreach and evangelization toward one's most primary relationships. Even if we—the author and readers—were to take a few moments to list our natural *oikos* relationships, we probably could come up with a list of twenty to twenty-five names, many of whom could be described as unchurched, inactive, or alienated. At St. Boniface, small groups do the evangelizing. It should be noted that in his famous work, *Converts, Drop-Outs, and Returnees,* sociologist Dean Hoge affirms the insight that the best, most effective evangelization is done through existing primary relationships.

There are other evangelical principles implicit in the OIKOS model. They are: multiplication and maximum influence. Multiplication refers to a peer-to-peer evangelizing wherein the one evangelized goes on to evangelize another, thus resulting in increasing membership.

Maximum influence refers to an ecclesial responsibility that a church body feels to reach as many persons as possible, and welcome them into some experience of church, either large group or cell group. More specifically, the St. Boniface community believes that if you have twenty people in an OIKOS cell group, you potentially have 400—for one of each of the twenty has an *oikos* of twenty. Another value to the OIKOS strategy is the natural follow-up implicit in the model. Follow-up to evangelization is not an artificial, alienating kind of effort, but part of being in a natural relationship.

For someone to make the commitment of time and energy that belonging to a small group entails, the Eivers team believes that there needs to be a process toward, or gradual immersion into, the group. That process is what they would call evangelization. Briefly, let us review what they see as the major steps of the process.

1. Helping or serving another. Entrance into the deeper parts of someone's life comes when we offer to help carry part of the heaviness of a burden or difficulty or problem that they are shouldering. Some would call this a state of preevangelization.

2. As a relationship builds between the active, practicing believer and the inactive or apathetic one, the active believer can begin, nonmanipulatively, to share his or her faith—in word and behavior.

3. Sharing faith may lead to questions on the part of the one being evangelized. The OIKOS evangelizer, in simple terms, answers religious, spiritual questions as best as he or she can.

4. In the unfolding of the evangelizing process, a person is invited to make a *commitment* to Christ and the church, and to begin to be *involved* in church life. Specifically, an invitation is given to belong to the small group that the OIKOS evangelizer belongs to.

5. The "neophyte," if you will, is assimilated into, incorporated into, the cell or small group.

6. Painstakingly, the small group stresses the relationship between the small group and the larger eucharistic assembly. The small-group member feels welcome—in both the cell group and the larger church.

7. The small group helps the new member to discern his or her charisms or gifts, and to get involved in ministry.

St. Boniface's system is not proselytizing; members do not seek to "steal sheep" who are actively involved in other churches. Rather OIKOS evangelization specifically targets the inactive, the alienated, the apathetic, or those who are "outside Christ," or spiritually unawakened.

The average size of a small group at St. Boniface is twelve members. We can see the multiplication-maximum influence principles at work in the process of cellular division. If through OIKOS evangelization groups begin to reach sixteen to twenty, cell leaders are encouraged to begin thinking about a split off, or beginning another small group.

The average time of most meetings of a group is ninety minutes, never longer than two hours. During that time period, the small group will sing, share stories from life or the week, share Scripture, share sound teaching, and pray. Each small-group meeting concludes with the small group forming a circle, with hands joined, for prayer. The circle, however,

Figure 3: Leadership Flow Chart

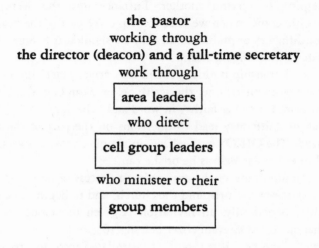

the pastor
working through
the director (deacon) and a full-time secretary
work through

area leaders

who direct

cell group leaders

who minister to their

group members

does not face inward, but rather outward—toward the doors and windows of the home the group meets in. This symbolic act stresses the evangelistic nature of the small groups. Each meeting closes with a ritualistic reminder to the members to reach-out, reach-into their natural *oikos,* to bring new members to the group, expand, and cellularly divide.

The flow chart of leadership at St. Boniface resembles the Cho-Hurston Korean model. It can be seen in Figure 3. While the word "area" is generally interpreted geographically, a person need not end up in an OIKOS group that is geographically near his or her home.

The teaching components are largely devised by the pastor and the director working from the need discernment done through area leaders and cell group leaders. Using the tools of the age, often the teaching is done through video cassette, which insures a kind of quality control to "the product." In addition, video now allows the pastor to come into the home, on occasion, of many more of his parishioners, using the medium of television.

The St. Boniface team regularly offers seminars on their style of small-community growth for the entire country, at their parish site. The address and phone number of the parish, and how to reach the staff, appear in the back of this book.

2. The Stage-by-Stage Evolution of Small Group Experiences at St. Elizabeth Seton's, Archdiocese of Detroit

What follows is largely based on personal interactions with Father Art Baranowski, who now works full-time for the national RENEW office, in the area of post-RENEW small-group development. Art worked for years in "re-imagining the parish" around small communities. After almost a decade at St. Elizabeth's, about 30 percent of the parish was in small groups. Those may sound like very disappointing statistics. But considering the increasing privatism, individualism, and success orientation that is rampant in our culture, 30 percent is not, in fact, too disappointing a figure. I would like to reflect on two aspects of Art's work: his experience of groups evolving in stages, and the importance he gives to leadership training. Details of his fine work can be found in three volumes by Art: *Creating Small Faith Communities, Praying Alone and Together,* and *Pastoring the Pastors.*

As small groups organically developed, Art was able—in hindsight—to notice three stages to their evolution. During the first stage the groups very much needed structured material. He chose the Genesis II program by Father Vince Dwyer. He mentions, however, that RENEW, or any other of the fine catechetical materials produced for small groups, are helpful. In stressing the need for structure and materials, Baranowski is expressing a truism about Catholic culture. Catholics have been socialized to be private and quiet about their faith. Religion and spirituality are up there with sex in being considered no one else's business. Structure and materials relieve some of the tension of getting to know each other.

A second stage of small-group development was the stage of persons becoming comfortable about praying with each other. Not only is talking about faith foreign to many Catholics, the intimacy of *faithing* with, or praying with others, also can be intimidating. Much time, then, was and is given in the Baranowski model to exposure to various styles of prayer. This modeling of prayer styles helps in something I have always found important in working with people: rather than imposing one style of spirituality, helping them to find what fits them best.

The safety of structure and programs, the experimenting with various prayer styles, gave birth to a third stage, groups having the faith maturity to need only the upcoming lectionary readings and some directed questions on which to base their sessions. The directed questions are prepared by the pastor, staff members, and pastoral facilitators, in dialogue.

A second striking thing about Baranowski's work is his emphasis on leadership training. A person considering and being considered for leadership in a small group attends a minimum of sixteen formation sessions, a yearly overnight retreat, and, after acceptance, monthly support group and business-oriented meetings. The latter are in addition to meeting with one's own small cell group. The person who eventually "pastors" the small group is called a "pastoral facilitator." The minimum commitment required for this ministry is two years. Through the process of discernment, some discover in training that they are not gifted for this particular ministry, but nonetheless still can *belong* to a small group.

Baranowski develops for his pastoral facilitators, indeed for the whole parish, a healthy ecclesiology. He stresses an *experiential* vision of church on four levels: the universal church (which indeed is the most remote), the local church of the diocese or archdiocese, *pastored* by the ordinary; the parish, shepherded by the bishop's delegate, the pastor; and the small cell group, *pastored* by trained pastoral facilitators.

One critique of the Baranowski model comes from the St. Boniface camp (Father Michael Eivers). Some of the Eivers team see the Baranowski model as too static, too self-nurturing, not evangelistic enough. They fail to see much of an OIKOS, reach-out dynamic in Baranowski's groups. Many, besides Father Baranowski, maintain that developing a small group requires a gradual building toward rapport, communication, and trust— the achieving of genuine chemistry that ought not to be trifled with once it is achieved. According to this line of thinking, a small group is almost too delicate an organism to use for evangelization. Eivers and others see small groups as *the* natural way to evangelize. The truth, I believe, lies somewhere in between.

3. Moving Missions from the Church to Homes and Neighborhoods

Father Thomas Maney, Sister Joan Gerads, Father James Schuer, Anna Chernugal, and others are among those responsible for propagating this unique model of small group, rooted also in neighborhood renewal. Known popularly as Parish Neighborhood Renewal Ministry (PNRM), the movement now publishes a regular newsletter from Ms. Chernugal's hometown of Hibbing, Minnesota. The seminal form of the movement is found in Gerad and Maney's missionary efforts in Chile. Gerad and Maney credit two Dominicans, Father Ralph Rogawski and Sister Helen Raycraft—both of the Dominican missionary team—for having shared the process with them. Through Maney and others, the movement reached the dioceses of Duluth and St. Cloud, and now has spread throughout the country.

PNRM teams, via the Hibbing, Minnesota, office, agree to come to a parish to spark the renewal movement. They speak at all Masses and conduct a parish information night to educate the congregation, en masse, about what is to happen. The team also prays and works daily with the parish staff. A section of the parish, a particular neighborhood, is selected as a site for the first endeavors at renewal. Homes in the area are visited by trained parishioners, who invite those visited to a spiritual experience in one of the neighbors' home. There follows a five-night mission, or retreat, in the home of a designated parishioner in the neighborhood. A neighborhood is usually comprised of twenty-five to sixty units.

The theme of each of the evenings is: the presence of Jesus in a troubled world; Jesus, healer—yesterday and today; personal encounter with Jesus; renewal in the Holy Spirit; and Christian community. The sessions last one and a half hours each evening. There are presentations, Scripture reading, song, prayers of petition and thanksgiving, and personal sharing.

The final evening is pivotal in this model. On the last evening an invitation is extended to those interested to continue after the mission as a small community. Time is spent in discernment—selection of "servant leaders" who will coordinate future meetings. Some in the group will go on to offer the mission in other sections of the parish, or in other neighborhoods. It is essential that the servant leaders of the various neighborhoods meet regularly to network and resource each other. Each small neighborhood group is free to shape and design its own style of being a community, as well as the frequency with which it will meet. With such a rich diversity of small-group styles, the meetings of networking servant leaders are exciting times for idea swapping.

The model mission is offered over and over again within a parish until as many neighborhoods as possible are covered, and as many small communities as possible are generated. More enfleshing of this exciting model can be found in *Basic Communities—A Practical Guide for Renewing Neighborhood Churches* by Father Thomas Maney and Sister Joan Gerads. The address for the renewal center in Hibbing is given at the end of this book.

4. The Diocese of Little Rock: Small Groups and Sacred Scripture

In *The Unchurched American 1988*, George Gallup studies and provides statistics on the growing alienation from mainline religion among traditional Protestantism, Catholicism, and Judaism. Increasingly people seem to want to claim a so-called religious heritage without being tied into a worshiping community. But Gallup and others who have studied evangelical proselytism recently have observed another phenomenon, a phenomenon that is almost paradoxical. In a nation that is becoming more privatized and individualistic, the religious movements that are the most popular are "high touch" or people-oriented. In frequent lectures that I have given around the country, I mention three dynamics that seem to be at the core of evangelical Christianity's success: heartfelt worship and preaching, personal outreach, and the possibility of meeting in a small group. Such small group experiences usually are heavily involved in the study of and prayer over Scripture.

Briefly, let us recall George Gallup's recommendations to the Christian churches in America: provide people with quality religious experiences rather than stressing the legal, bureaucratic sides of church; evangelize families rather than just focusing on children; start proactive reach-out campaigns for the inactive and unchurched; initiate small communities in parishes, anchored in Scripture study and scriptural prayer.

With many Catholics responding to the high-touch, small group, scriptural emphasis of evangelical churches, the diocese of Little Rock, Arkansas, set out to create a process that would provide searching Catholics and others quality opportunities for small communities and Scripture study. Before examining the Little Rock Scripture Study model, let us reflect briefly on a healthy, nonfundamentalist approach to sacred Scripture.

Whenever I am asked to address groups of persons who are about to become involved in Scripture study, I like to share some biases or convictions that I have about studying or praying Scripture:

1. Fundamentalists or literalists stress the literal inerrancy of each passage of Scripture. Fundamentalist-literalists, often in a simplistic interpretation of Scripture, run the risk of missing the meaning and message of a given passage.

2. Rather than fundamentalism or literalism, the *contextual* approach to Scripture unlocks its fullest, most profound, meaning. Contextualists

seek the *context* of a given passage. Contextualists ask such questions as: When was the passage written? By whom? For whom? What type of literary devices were employed? These and other questions dig out a more in-depth analysis of Scripture, and consequently more of the truth of Scripture.

3. In a contextualist approach, *exegesis* is valued. Exegesis involves using footnotes, introductions, and commentaries, to engage in a movement backward, uncovering, in the process, the original message of the author for his/her day.

4. Exegesis is a kind of science, while *hermeneutics* is more of an art form. Hermeneutics, through prayer, imagination, and conversation, is a *movement forward* to find the possible meaning of a given passage for the contemporary age.

5. Scripture is best studied and prayed in community. Scripture ought not to be interpreted from an overprivatized posture. Rather Scripture comes alive most in relationships and in relationship to the tradition of the church.

6. Each person approaches Scripture with a subjective filter, or personal bias, that can be quite healthy. But that subjective posture needs to be balanced with other realities, like the importance of exegesis and hermeneutics.

7. There is not one biblical vision of theology. Rather the Bible is a whole library of life visions and theologies that can be understood only through study and exegesis.

8. The Bible is a tool, an instrument for and toward personal and communal conversion, leading to encounter with God in prayer, and helping persons to share their own faith with each other.

9. We need to refrain from bibliolatry, or idol worship of the Bible. The Bible is not God, but rather an instrument of faith.

10. Nonetheless we need to have a profound reverence for the Scriptures as a book of paradigmatic stories, images, and metaphors that mirror or reflect our personal stories and faith journeys.

Now back to the Little Rock series. Through the painstaking work of Fathers Jerome Kodell and Richard Oswald, and Deacon Johnson Mattingly, the Little Rock Scripture Study office now has at least fourteen programs based on different books of the Bible, with accompanying print, audio, and visual (video) aids. Some of the programs are now also in Spanish. A gathering of small communities around Scripture happens weekly, for eight to ten weeks perhaps twice a year. The coordinators suggest that groups begin with the Acts of the Apostles, the account of the birth of the church. A meeting lasts about an hour and a half. For a few moments, all gather in a large group in a big gathering space. After prayer, the small groups go to various parts of the parish center for small-group sharing.

The small-group sharing is encased in a unique dynamic called conversational prayer. The group leader or assistant leader asks the group to stand, and if comfortable with it, to join hands. The first step of conversational prayer is to simply imagine Jesus—however one may visualize him—present within the small group. Step two of conversational prayer is for individuals to offer praise and thanks for gifts and graces received. The group then sits down and shares reflections on journal questions that cover one or two chapters of the particular book being studied. Group members should not come to the small group unprepared. They are to read and pray over the assigned passages and then to journal answers to questions about what they have read and prayed. This "homework," if you will, lasts about twenty minutes a day. After about fifty minutes of such sharing, the leaders conclude the small-group time by engaging in steps three and four of conversational prayer. In step three, small-group members are invited to offer specific petitions for themselves. In step four, the group prays for others who are in need of prayer. The entire evening closes with a lecture on the passage just discussed, with all groups meeting again in a large room. The lecture can be given by a staff member, a competent lay person, or can be experienced through audio or video tape, distributed by the central office.

The genius of the Little Rock program is that it blends competent Scripture study skills with faith sharing and shared prayer in small groups. The program can be arranged so as to be done in homes, and aids for developing a children's ministry are also provided.

Much like RENEW, the Little Rock Scripture Study program is of particular value to parishes just beginning small communities. They provide both structure and materials that newcomers to small groups often need.

5. Chicago Parish Spirituality

A group of parishes that had finished RENEW approached me, as the director of the Office for Evangelization in the archdiocese of Chicago, to help them develop some material for continuing small groups. What we took on for the next three years was the production of a series entitled

Parish Spirituality. Other duties have prevented me from continuing the production of materials for the series. The books are still available through the Chicago Office. *Parish Spirituality* was rooted in several convictions:

1. Rather than ascribing topics of interest to adults, we asked parishes involved to survey their small groups about the kind of topics they would like to discuss in groups. Discussion aids were then designed and written to address real, felt adult needs.

2. The upcoming Sunday readings become a key part of the prayer of the groups. Articles were written to aid homilists in preparing to preach on passages that many small groups had already shared during the week. Thus, small groups, Sunday liturgy, and homilists connected at least ideally.

3. Artists on the parish spirituality team put together replicable symbols for environmental use at liturgy, bulletin covers, or buttons to be worn by parishioners.

4. One woman whose expertise was child and family catechesis made suggestions on how the themes studied in small groups, preached and written about on weekends, symbolically celebrated and worn—could also be brought to children and families. For six six-week sessions (3 years of 2 blocks of six weeks), she worked at making suggestions on how to translate the small-group theme to children both in CCD and parochial schools, and also how to provide parents with suggestions on how to talk with their children about topics in the domestic church or family.

Thus, the key elements in *Parish Spirituality* were:

—adult catechesis based on needs
—connection with the lectionary
—support for preachers in connecting small groups with the lectionary
—model bulletin articles
—liturgical environmental suggestions and logos
—CCD-school connections
—suggestions for family ministry.

The themes developed over six-week periods, as discerned by need discernment of adults involved in either RENEW or other parish activities, were:

1. The Parish: A Praying Community—an overview on various styles and ways to pray
2. Sacraments Alive! a history of the sacraments as well as suggestions for a contemporary understanding and living of them today

3. Jesus: Teacher, Lord, and Savior: a summary of the scriptural views of who Jesus was from the perspectives of Matthew, Mark, Luke, John, and Paul
4. Kingdom Responses: an analysis of morality as responsibility for the quality of life and the reign of God
5. Improving Relationships: nuts-and-bolts skills for marriage, parenting, or other significant relationship
6. The Parish: Community of Communities: essentially a how-to series—models of how to be small communities without someone's generating materials for the parish all the time. These six weeks tried to teach the internal discipline of how to be a small community.

Financial backing and time constraints forced me as editor to do volume six, and then stop production. With volume six I essentially was saying, "It is time to take the guard wheels off the bicycle, so that you can learn to ride the bicycle of a 'parish as small communities' yourselves." I really valued the far-reaching effects of connecting Sunday liturgy, bulletin articles and covers, children's religious education, family education, art and environment, and small communities—all around common themes for six weeks, twice a year. I am proud to report that although the many parishes involved no longer receive materials from me, they have continued the learned discipline of small groups integrated with other parish efforts. The parishes involved reported a "great leveling" effect in having so many in the parish pray and study around the same issues—issues named by the persons themselves as needs.

Like the Little Rock Scripture Study program, *Parish Spirituality*, the adult, small-community component, required preparation. While the discussion questions were largely for use in the small group, a participant would have little to share if he or she did not first read a brief article on the week's theme, as well as relevant Scripture passages.

Currently, *Parish Spirituality* sits on my book shelves, crying out for revision, updating, and accommodation to all three cycles of the lectionary, so that the materials could be used during any of the lectionary cycles. I so believe in small groups, and the expansive integration of efforts that many parishes experienced that used *Parish Spirituality*, that I intend to get to those revisions and updatings very soon.

Following are some of the logos used during *Parish Spirituality* seasons.

SACRAMENTS
ALIVE!

A Praying Community

CHRISTIAN
RELATIONSHIPS

10
Leadership

In all the models studied in this book—Cho-Hurston's, Baranowski's, Little Rock Scripture Study, Parish Neighborhood Renewal, Parish Spirituality, as also Latin American and African models (Lumko, the Better World Movement)—*leadership* is a key factor. Whether in these models, or a more simple, less demanding one like that described in the chapter on neighborhood pastoring, the raising up and training of good leaders is a necessity. Whether in home visitation or small-group facilitation, the nonordained baptized share in the pastoring of the faithful. While I hold to my conviction that we indeed need more pastors, I am also convinced that the *right lay leaders, properly trained,* are also a necessity.

We need to keep in mind the reality of *charisms,* and call people to training and then ministry, based on charisms. The question before us as we struggle to animate small communities is, Who has the charism for small-group leadership? Only one who seems to be called and gifted (and then trained) for it should be placed in such a position.

One of the unique skills that a group leader needs is the openness to engage in healthy self-critique and group critique. Often a marriage gets into trouble because a couple fails to be honest about what is truly going on between the two of them. In much the same way, group relationships can sour if the group cannot tell the leader either how he or she is doing, or how the group experience is going for him, her, them.

From a Business Perspective

Some of the most life-giving insights about people, relationships, motivation, and groups in recent years has come from the writing of Tom

Peters and his associates *(In Search of Excellence; A Passion for Excellence; Thriving on Chaos).* In his many articles and talks, as well as books, Peters laments the decline of the quality of business, labor, and productivity in America. But he pinpoints the cause of malaise in American business on the level of the relational. People produce a poor product, which Americans increasingly do not buy, in deference to a foreign import, because they are not excited or encouraged in their work. Leadership at any level of a business, he says, is essentially the work of motivation and encouragement. He has a wonderful definition of a leader: "A leader is a fanatic with a vision, who coaches and encourages those around him or her." In ecclesial terms, good pastor figures (on a staff level) are visionaries who excite the nonordained baptized into enthusiasm over sharing in pastoring.

Peters contends that good leaders in our institutions, either a staff member or someone in lay leadership, divest themselves of hierarchical symbols of power. They try to be inclusive in terms of getting as many as possible involved in the mission of the corporation or group. They manage more by presence and encouragement than by distance and indirect communication.

Peters's key words about good leadership are: vision, passion, nonhierarchical, inclusive, coaching, getting as many involved at their own rate and level as possible. These are notions that ordained, professed, degreed, and volunteers ought to take to heart.

Specific Leadership Qualities

International experience has shown that what are needed in a small-group leader are not highly developed theological skills. In the small groups that I have helped animate, I have spent much more time in sharpening skills of:

1. good body language for communication
2. active listening
3. how to ask informational questions
4. how to ask open-ended questions that elicit life stories and faith sharing
5. how to confront without putting another down
6. empathy and the ability to communicate it

7. affirming others
8. drawing quiet persons out of the woodwork—those that want to come out
9. a comfort with silence
10. a rehearsed flexibility that is ready to try other questions, or go down another road, or follow the group's lead, if what is prepared is not working
11. a love of people
12. a desire to be helpful rather than to impress
13. the ability to handle anger, tears, hurt, in self or in others
14. the ability to gently redirect talkers who hold the group captive
15. a growing ability to pray with others
16. a relatively current knowledge of faith and church matters
17. an ability to show humanity and vulnerability
18. a willingness to share faith, when appropriate
19. time—both for ongoing training and support of fellow leaders
20. a discipline to respect the agreed upon schedule and length of meetings

Much of the above can be modeled and practiced in training; but it is fine-tuned in *doing*. Again, in small groups there are diverse ministries. No one ought to feel ashamed if his or her charism is not leadership. The charism of leadership includes some of the skills and qualities discussed above.

Before I preach, I quietly ask God's help in three areas: "Lord, help me to feel good about myself (for fear and poor self-image can get in the way of allowing myself to be used as an instrument). Help me to love these people (love them, want to help them—not impress them). Help me to give witness to you (that you, God, are real, and a therapeutic force in my life)."

This rehearsal prayer seems to properly motivate and dispose me for the ministry of preaching. While my prayer style need not be thrust on others, prayer is one of the most important ways for a small-group leader to prepare for the next meeting.

11

The RCIA as Model for Basic Christian Communities and Adult Faith Formation

Anyone who has studied the Rite of Christian Initiation for Adults, engaged in the process, served as a minister in the process, or read the 1988 revised rite of the RCIA knows that a great deal of what has been advocated and encouraged so far in this book happens in the RCIA experience. Using the revised rite, we are told that there are four target populations in our culture for the dynamics of the catechumenate: pure catechumens, or those never baptized; baptized Christians now seeking full communion with the Roman Catholic Church; those baptized but uncatechized; and children of catechetical age seeking sacraments of initiation. What happens to persons who comprise these subpopulations, as they journey through the catechumenate, is essentially what a small Christian community is about. Put another way, small communities help the rest of us experience on a regular basis what those in the RCIA journey experience. We briefly study the RCIA, then, to round out our understanding of small communities, and to make a transition to the next section of this book.

A Reflection on the Sacramental Life

The catechumenate must be understood up against the context of our evolving sacramental system. The word first used by the postresurrection communities to speak of the rituals of initiation—the water bath of baptism, the consignation with chrism (later confirmation), and eu-

79

charist—is *mysterion* (Greek) or *mysterium* (Latin). The rituals that expressed immersion into the paschal event, the life of the Trinity, and life in community were called *mysteries*. Around the year 210 A.D., Tertullian, one of the fathers of the church, used the word *sacramentum* to refer to those rituals. We are familiar with a more contemporary connotation of the word *sacramentum*, the connotation of a sacrament being a visible sign of something invisible. When Tertullian used the word *sacramentum*, he had quite a different understanding of it. Technically, the word, borrowed from the Roman military, meant to the people of Tertullian's day, *to vow*. Soldiers took a *sacramentum*, a vow to live and die for Caesar. Tertullian felt the strength of the word *sacramentum* was congruent with what the rites of Christian initiation should be—an experience of vowing to live and die for Jesus and the community in which his risen presence was so manifest.

In the many stages that comprise our sacramental evolution, the era of the golden age of the catechumenate, from the second to the fourth centuries, was one in which sacramental rituals were expressive of entrance into community. To return to an earlier theme, the catechumenate—then and now—was a process of word, ritual, and life-sharing in which participants entered into egalitarian communities, or communities of equals, mythic or special mystical time, and the divine life. The symbols and rituals of the process, then and now, especially touch the imagination and influence dominant images in peoples' lives. The catechumenate diminished in popular experience, from the fourth to the seventh centuries, with some of the emphasis on conversion shifting to formation in seminaries, convents, monasteries, and religious life.

It is important to take note of what is happening internationally to the RCIA, through the influences of the North American Forum on the Catechumenate and other organizations.

1. More and more the Sunday Scripture readings are becoming central to the evangelization-catechetical process. This is a dramatic shift from catechetical aids to a Scripture-based catechesis. This emphasis does not preclude making other reading material available, or offering lectures or teaching. But much of the time now in catechumenal sessions is spent "breaking open the word," using methods similar to the "look, listen, love" model discussed earlier. This new orientation is rooted in the conviction that Scripture is a book of paradigmatic stories, images, and persons. In the paradigmatic story, participants find their own stories. Scripture is used in helping people name their meeting of God in ordinary

experience. The centering on Scripture also raises catechetical questions that catechists can do their best to research and answer.

2. The importance of the sponsor has been retrieved, lending a tone of real mentoring, befriending, personalism, relational bonding, and guidance to the whole process.

3. The catechumenal community, made up of those taking the journey as well as the ministering community, stands in a dialogical relationship with the worshiping community. The catechumenal community is a sign and reminder of conversion and community to the larger congregation. The larger community is a sign and reminder of conversion and community to the small catechumenal community.

Thus a full, vital implementation of the revised RCIA rite is perhaps one of the best starting points in educating the congregation about the nature and importance of small Christian communities.

The antithesis of the vision of conversion and sacraments present in the RCIA is the view of sacraments as "holy things" that one accumulates as Catholic culture so dictates. This vision, a progressive distortion of medieval theology and praxis, has severed the connection between sacraments and conversion, community, discernment, vowing, and responsible membership in ecclesial bodies. Unfortunately this latter Tridentine view is still permeating Catholics minds and souls—in the pews and in the higher circles of ecclesial leadership.

Learning from the RCIA about Small Communities

The revised rite teaches that the parish needs to be in an ongoing state of precatechumenate or evangelization. In other words, a parish does not passively wait for potential new members to come to it and then inform them to come back next fall when "the program starts again." Rather, certain community members are gifted and called, in an ongoing way, to do outreach and evangelization. The OIKOS model that we analyzed encourages people in small groups to be an ongoing posture of precatechumenate or evangelization. Small groups, catechumenal in nature, are never exclusive, but always inclusive and inviting in nature.

The RCIA has many dynamics and principles that are instructive to people involved in small-group work. Like catechumenal groups, small groups are characterized by the following:

1. are not programs, but processes;
2. are about conversion;
3. stress *koinonia* or community over individualism and anonymity, as the medium for church and ministry;
4. realize that conversion and communities take time;
5. focus on adults (with children being socialized into groups of strong adult faith);
6. realize sacraments are about vowing and revowing, and are not "holy things";
7. discern charisms for ministry, realizing that even the small church requires diverse ministries;
8. always stay connected with the larger assembly;
9. live a spirituality that is paschal—passage, in nature—with Christ from life through death to new life;
10. value *discernment:* watching, waiting, reflecting, praying, seeking critique or affirmation from others;
11. see storytelling, or life sharing, as vital for group life;
12. experience revelation, not as history, nor just ecclesial doctrine, but rather coming to new awareness over and over again of God leaving clues of self-manifestation in our lives.

Using a Catechumenal Model to Gradually Transform a Parish Toward Communities

If there is truth and life in some of these catechumenal principles and dynamics, then small communities could begin to gradually emerge soon in most parishes, if there would be gentle restructuring to insure that the following ministries be done in the manner of community and according to RCIA principles and dynamics:

—ongoing precatechumenate
—catechumens seeking initiation
—the already baptized seeking full communion
—the baptized, yet uncatechized, seeking active membership
—children of catechetical age seeking sacraments of initiation with parental support and the aid of catechists and sponsors
.—ongoing adult education based on discerned needs

—families in faith formation leading to first eucharist and first reconciliation
—pastoral care to the poor, sick, homeless
—welcoming newcomers
—marriage preparation and ongoing enrichment
—full cycle youth evangelization
—the evangelization of young adults

Small Groups in Embryo

As I briefly mentioned in another book, *The Evangelizing Parish,* we have small groups just waiting to happen, if only we took already existing ministries and organizations and gave them a more communal-RCIA tonality. Rather than just running to *tasks* all the time, let those in parish ministry minister out of the experience of prayer, Scripture sharing, life sharing, and journey that constitute small Christian communities and RCIA groups. I am talking here also of lectors, ushers, ministers of communion, the women's organization, the men's organization, and so on.

As mentioned earlier, parish governance is another area for allowing community to seep in. We ought to strike the language of teams, boards, and councils from our vocabulary and speak of phenomena like the religious education community, the worship community, the youth ministry community, the finances and administration community, and the pastoral care community. Such organisms would be made up of discerned leaders in each cluster of parish ministry. These smaller leadership communities would in turn discern representatives to meet regularly with parish staff, and representatives of OIKOS or neighborhood communities in a parish leadership community—a renewed version of the parish council. All these departments of parish governance—in addition to their immediate tasks—would pray, share life, and share Scripture also. The parish leadership community would be charged with long-range discernment and planning regarding the ongoing spiritual direction and evangelization of the entire parish, the small groups, and the ministering groups.

Part II

Adulthood

12

Adult Faith

The first part of this book about small faith communities was really about adults, awakening to faith, growing in faith, supporting each other in faith. In this second section, we will examine more closely—not just the dynamics and composition of small groups—but also the dynamics of adulthood and faith in the adult years. Both concepts, adulthood and faith, are increasingly elusive and difficult to understand, for they bring us back to the realms of imagination and dominant image-shifting, which can be described, even rationally defended, but rarely explained well. We will begin with perhaps the more elusive of the two notions—faith.

In a fine talk at a recent National Catholic Education Association gathering, Sister Joan Chittister described the kind of faith that ideally Catholic religious education efforts should try to foster. She spoke of *relational faith,* a faith anchored in a personal relationship with God, through Jesus, in the Holy Spirit. Perhaps the church of previous decades was a bit short on this type of faith. But the next model, we were good at propagating: *intellectual faith,* a body of truths that we knew, knew about, and could articulate. Perhaps recent catechetical efforts have been weak here, producing a generation of religious illiterates who neither understand nor can explain (and therefore pass on) their traditions. Sister Chittister added: we have come to an age that cries out for another approach to faith: *performative faith.* Faith is a matter of doing, living, behaving in a certain way. Specifically, we are called to behavioralize the values of the kingdom or reign of God. Faith cries out for enfleshment in deeds of mercy and justice.

I would add to Sister Joan's fine analysis a fourth type of faith we need to foster: *imaginative faith.* We are invited to *know* the Lord, to *know about* the Lord and the church, to *live* our faith. But we are also invited to *articulate for ourselves* what are the dominant intrapsychic images out of which we live our lives, what are the seductive images of the culture, what are the (at times dysfunctional) images of the institutional church. Naming these, we are invited via evangelizing-catechizing communities, also to the dominant images out of which Jesus Christ lived his life. He called that synthesis of convictions, images, divine power, and grace "the reign of God." We are returning here to the theme with which we began this book: *imagination*. To live from his images necessitates an often painful transition from personal intrapsychic, cultural, and ecclesial images, to invest in kingdom images.

Adult faith is at once relational, intellectual, performative, and imaginative. Perhaps this last dimension is the most powerful and influential in our lives, yet heretofore the least talked about or studied. Change can occur at any time on one or more levels. We call it, when it happens, conversion or transformation.

Karl Rahner wrote that conversion takes on no one size or shape; neither do the various kinds of conversion necessarily flow in any ordered sequence. There is basic religious conversion, which is awakening to mystery present in human experience. This is theistic conversion wherein one names the mystery as "personal God." People can likewise experience Christic conversion, which is an awakening to Jesus Christ as the way to God and truth. In ecclesial conversion, people awaken to a need for church, community. In moral conversion, changed hearts and minds begin to express themselves in changed behavior. In intellectual conversion, a person begins to see and experience the truth in other religious traditions as well as one's own. The complexity of people sharing conversion experiences is evident in Rahner's breakdown. Individuals do not necessarily even mean the same things when they talk about conversion.

One of the principles discussed about small communities and also the RCIA was relative to *revelation*—that God leaves clues of self-manifestation in present experience. That principle is intimately connected to this discussion of conversion. When God apparently breaks into adults' lives, it is rarely in church. It is rather in human experience: illness, health, joy, sadness, moral search, sin, success, disappointment, love, divorce, death. These are the human experiences that become thresholds or springboards to a new or first experience of God. Yet Edward Braxton reflecting on this mysterious process in the *Wisdom Community* wrote that human experiences like the ones mentioned above throw some persons *not* into a conversion process but rather a nose dive of agnosticism, atheism, or idolatry. What is it that prompts some to find God in human experiences and others to find only a dark abyss? Braxton feels that the difference is the presence of believers, persons of faith, who "walk with" someone especially in a struggle experience. Faith-filled presence with, prayer with, faith with, helps searching, struggling persons with the leap of the imagination, which is essentially faith. Here we begin to see the connection between growing faith and small groups. The small intentional community is certainly a mileau in which support, nurturance, and guidance can aid in the journey of faith.

In discussing ministering to the young adult population, Sharon Parks in *The Critical Years* lends support to what I am suggesting. Parks feels that essentially what "would-be young adult believers" need most is *mentoring*. Mentoring refers to a process of a "seeker" relating to, interacting with, someone who has both vulnerability and proven existential authority. In the mix of the relationship, the mentor's inner world, dreams, and values begin to be appropriated and uniquely reshaped by the person being mentored. If the church is to be relevant to young adult lives, writes Parks, it must mentor with credibility. The failure to mentor toward the reign of God, or the commonwealth of God, as the author restates it, will result in young adults being mentored by the values of the narcissistic, consumer world around them. She is quite insightful when she says people cannot help but be mentored. Someone, something will mentor you, me, everyone.

Mentoring is at the core of the catechumenal process. It is key in preevangelization and evangelization, in which, through relationships, people enter each others' worlds, and the evangelizer—either in word or deed—gives witness to a transforming relationship he or she has with the Lord.

We are getting ahead of ourselves in discussing specific subpopulations of adults, but discussion of young adults and mentoring gives rise to memories of reading about and hearing what some dioceses in Australia have done recently in ministering to young adults. Those with the charge to minister to young adults in some parts of Australia have more or less thrown up their hands and said "Let's face it—the water has been poured, but most young adults in this country are unevangelized and unconverted." This gave rise to the *Toward Discipleship* process of small-group meetings in homes. Young adults in late adolescence and the twenties meet in small communities with mentoring figures somewhat older than they—with people in their thirties and forties who have had conversion experiences. The model is based on the RCIA, and invites the young adults involved to progressively move toward a commitment to Christ and the church, and then active, responsible membership in the parish community.

Adult Transformation: Turning or Grasped?

For years, the popular wisdom regarding adult faith moments or conversion was that through human experience one had an awakening, a breakthrough to God, and a consequent *metanoia*, or turning toward God. I have come to see and experience the process in a different way. Actually Paul Tillich described it in these terms years ago. He described conversion as first having been *grasped* by mystery, by God. Paul, for example, and the two on the way to Emmaus, were at first grasped by a "more." After being grasped, or convicted of (convinced by) the experience, they consequently *turned*.

This might seem like so much minutia to the reader, but it really is a very important shift in vision concerning conversion. The "we turn first" theory stresses our will power. The "God grasping first" theory suggests that conversion is not so much our willfill breakthrough to God, but rather God's breakthrough into our lives. This breakthrough comes in a place, or experience, of poverty, brokenness, or vulnerability. Thus Jesus lauds some human powerlessness experiences in the Sermon on the Mount (Matthew), or the Sermon on the Plain (Luke); for they are proven entrance points for the spirit of the holy to enter our lives. "Blest are we" in these apparently dark moments, for deprived of false security, we are liberated for and gifted with real security: the divine presence, grace. The tension or balance between being grasped and will power in the conversion process is expressed well by Dr. Gerald May, in the book *Will and Spirit*. In that study, he describes the conversion dialectic as a delicate balance or interplay between willfullness (will power) and willingness, an openness to "being taken" by someone greater than ourselves. This is the experience of spiritual surrender.

In another study, *Addiction and Grace,* May describes our consumer culture as essentially *addicted* or overattached in life-robbing relationships with things, values, or people. With Anne Wilson Schaef and Sr. Diane Fassel, May would concur that most of us are ensnared in some addiction. The opposite of the addictive life-style is the admission of how powerless and chaotic one's life has become, and in the admission of poverty, a surrender to the gentle sway of grace, or divine power.

In his fine study, *Experiential Religion,* as well as in his teaching, Richard J. Niebuhr speaks of the Tillichian "grasped" experience in other metaphorical language. He speaks of the "God-breaking into our life" experience as the experience of shipwreck. Life's mysteries literally toss us into the cold, chaotic waters of living. We feel we are drowning, over our heads, dying. Yet amid this chaos, there is another experience, the experience of being washed ashore by a power greater than the self. Notice Neibuhr does not speak of swimming ashore. No—the experience is that of being washed ashore. Finding oneself on shore, a person is filled with gladness and amazement that he or she not only still is, but has been transformed. Maturing faith is learning to trust the process, for it surely will happen again and again.

The Void and the Holy

A study that has a profound impact on me—which many, including myself, found difficult to read—is *The Transforming Moment* by James Loder. Using personal examples from his own life, as well as reviewing scriptural models, he speaks of conversion as "transforming moments," and "convictional experiences." Loder describes the process. In the *world,* one enters a *void* experience (darkness, emptiness in life). It is natural to try to *avoid the void;* but entering the void experience, one begins to sense the holy present in the void. The imagination, not the intellect, scans possibilities for interpreting life from the perspective of being in the void. The scanning leads to the leap of the imagination toward the holy, and a whole new reinterpretation of one's life.

The process does not end there, writes Loder. Like Paul going to Ananias after his conversion, people who have had such experiences go to others for confirmation—in a sense, "tell me that I am not crazy, that perhaps I indeed met God." After the confirmation experience, a person seeks a *culture* that fosters and nurtures the transformational experience. That culture, writes Loder, is both community and its rituals or liturgy. Thus we return to the issue of community, large and small, and its importance in fostering adult faith.

Figure 4: Stages of Development

	Erik Erikson on Human Development	James Fowler on Faith Development	Iris Ford on Self-Transcendence*	Lawrence Kohlberg on Moral Development
infancy (0 to 1½)	trust vs. mistrust	undifferentiated faith	simple faith (to 6 months) imitative faith (to 1 year)	premoral stage
early childhood (2–6)	autonomy vs. shame/doubt initiative vs. guilt	intuitive, projective faith (importance of stories, symbols)	literal faith (2–5 years)	heteronomous morality (subject to external laws and imposition of norms)
childhood (7–13)	industry vs. inferiority	mythic, literal faith (accepting a tradition, relying on adults)	learned faith (6–11 years)	instrumental exchange (doing good to get what one wants)
adolescence (13–21)	identity vs. identity confusion	synthetic, conventional faith (pulling it all together, conforming, not critical)	relational faith (12–14 years) searching faith (15–21 years)	morality based on need for mutual interpersonal relationships
young adulthood (21–35)	intimacy vs. isolation	Individuative-reflective faith (critical thinking; search for *owned* faith)	reflective faith (22–29 years) serving faith (30–39 years)	morality based on social system or conscience
adulthood (36–60)	generativity vs. stagnation	conjunctive faith (postcritical acceptance of tradition, recognizing limits as well as strengths of other traditions)	suffering faith (40–55 years) liberating faith (55–65 years)	morality based on social contracts and individual rights
maturity (60+)	integrity vs. despair	universalizing faith (community or solidarity with all beings and the universe)	renewing faith (65–75 years) resurrection faith (75+)	universal ethical principles

*Birth to age 21 is the process of self-actualization; 22–75 is the true goal of adulthood: self-transcendence

The Critique on "The Stages"

The emphases in this book on imagination, leaping hearts vs. rational intellect, shifting dominant images, being grasped even before one turns, stand in bold contrast to the theories about conversion popular the last ten to fifteen years. Developmental psychology has certainly influenced our understanding of faith growth and moral development. We have spoken of the stages of moral and faith development as invariant, epigenetic (or building one upon the other)—and how many who claim to be believers are unfortunately trapped or stalled at rather immature stages of development. Some of those stages, laid in parallel positions to each other, are diagramed in Figure 4.

The developmentalists are not to be dismissed. A cursory view of their work reveals immediately apparent truth, truth we have all experienced. I find myself, however, now in a middle position between the developmentalists and those who emphasize the "grasped, imaginative, leaping heart" nuances of conversion. Loder contends that the axis of imaginative transformation is much more congruent with reality, with what really happens in people's lives, than it is with a sort of lockstep progression through stages. The stages may provide some helpful language to describe the point at which people arrive, but the process is deeply internal and imaginative. In fact, Loder says that in a transforming moment, or convictional experience, a person can jump more than one stage at a time, yet assimilating the wisdom inherent in the stages nonetheless. What I like about Tillich, Loder, May, Rahner, and Braxton is their restoration of *mystery* in the process of conversion, that we *turn* after being *grasped*. To lose this perspective results in a pleasant psychological-sounding form of fundamentalistism, wherein we sound like we control the mystery.

Where the developmentalists and the others concur is again in the area of the importance of mentors, or faithful others, who help in this journey. Fowler and Kolhberg contend that it is only upon the discovery of the inadequacy of the status of one stage that a person is even open to the possibility of moving to another. When the opportunity arrives, it is usually the influence of another person a stage ahead of that person that nudges him or her to the next stage. The communal impact on conversion is again reiterated.

James Fowler, in his later works, and certainly Iris Ford in her study *Life Spiral: The Faith Journey,* present the stages of spiritual development in nonhierarchical terms. They re-image the stages as a process spiraling ever more deeply into mystery. Ford builds on Robert Kegan's model of gradual, stage-by-stage self-actualization, as described in his *The Evolving Self.* Kegan describes the process of growth as a kind of embeddedness in one state, a gaining of homeostasis therein, then the loss of that, and a decentration or emergence into another stage, all ideally moving toward self-actualization. Ford, building on Kegan's spiral, sees the goal of adult development to be more than self-actualization. It is, rather, self-transcendence, a discovery of the importance of God and relationships. Paradoxically self-actualization is only found through self-transcendence. Ford's suggestion is certainly antithetical to the wisdom of the age and the culture.

With Gabriel Moran, and others, I am cautious about a possible elitism in the stages. I often say that persons my parents' age are at a more profound stage of faith than I, though they could never explain it or even understand it from the perspective of contemporary developmentalists. Some of the empirical-sounding language of the stage theorists excludes language that is more relevant to and congruent with images of the kingdom. We do not hear talk of sanctity, holiness, prayerfulness, compassion, and the like, in some of the work of developmentalists. It may be implied, but is not very clear.

Other critical thinkers have added other concerns about the validity of the stages. Are they exclusive of certain racial and socio-economic groups? In other words, would African Americans find themselves on Kohlberg's chart, or on Fowler's? I am not referring exclusively to language or terminology, but rather to experience. Do the stages of morality and faith development reflect the experience of an African American, especially one shackled by the chains of inner-city poverty, homelessness, or some other injustice? In a similar vein, does the analytical, conceptual, cerebral language of the stages reflect the experiences of the Hispanic immigrant who comes to North America with a high sensitivity to the Spirit-world, an earth-bound spirituality, one that is also deeply embedded in a sense of extended family? A similar question could be asked about Asians, Christian or those of Eastern religions, whose spirituality is much more right-brain oriented than that represented by the left-brained stages.

The Feminist Critique

Perhaps the loudest voice in critiquing the stage mentality is that of Dr. Carol Gilligan *(In a Different Voice),* and others of her persuasion. Quite insightfully, Dr. Gilligan suggests that perhaps much of the developmentalists' work is too influenced by and skewed toward the male world. The language and imagery of even as far back as Erikson's theory, she says, reflect male strivings and values. In fact, much to Gilligan's annoyance, some experts, using Kohlberg's categories, found women to be less prone to move toward the "advanced" stages of moral development—as men more frequently do. Some studies revealed that women seem "stopped" at Kohlberg's stage 3, a morality based on the development of happy interpersonal relationships, one that could be nonreflectively labeled adolescent or preadolescent.

In response, feminists would say the stages are based on movement into and through male values. Male values are held up as ideals, with little heed to the often misunderstood innerworld of the female. The stages have within them the implied male values of individualism, becoming a strong self, separation from others, and success.

The reason why females may "rate low" in such a schema is that they operate out of a different set of dominant images. Hierarchy is not only the dominant image of what Boff calls traditionalistic ecclesiology; it is also the prime metaphor for the entire male way of being and doing. Some of this may have mellowed a bit in recent years. But by and large, men are still "ascending ladders" while women are always spinning and weaving webs—relational webs. The so-called preadolescent and adolescent morality based on maintaining good relationships, rather than a so-called lower stage of morality according to rational principles, is not in fact a situation of women arrested in a stage of lesser development. No, it is rather the feminine orientation toward morality and life situations based on the criterion of the relational vs. the fierce individuation and individualism in males. Gilligan and her associates firmly believe that men and women in our culture operate out of a different set of values, hear different inner voices, in effect speak different languages. The great challenge inherent in her work for men and women—either in small groups or in marriage and family life—is to explore and come to understand each other's worlds, each other's inner frames of reference.

For example, Gilligan feels the greatest fear over the years for men has been intimacy. The research of Dr. Frank Pitman, a marriage counselor for over twenty-five years, concurs with Gilligan's findings. In analyzing the phenomenon of infidelity in marriage, Pitman found that in fact men were the most frequent abusers of marriage vows, the most likely to become involved in extramarital affairs, which notoriously dynamites stable relationships. Contradicting the popular wisdom that men turn to affairs because of an unsatisfactory relationship with their spouses, Pitman states that experience has shown him that men turn to affairs because their marriages have reached a new point or turn requiring a deeper commitment to intimacy and longevity in the relationship, and they simply are afraid to do so. "The affair" becomes a sideshow that preempts that deeper intimacy.

Gilligan says the greatest fear women have had over the years is the fear of success. Again this may have mellowed in recent years, but Gilligan suggests that successful women, increasingly taking on the trappings of male individuation, fear the separation and violated relationships that rugged male individualism and success require. Thus, rather than choosing success, women will often choose a more highly relational mode of living.

A more recent feminist analysis of male-skewed society is found in the *Lost in the Land of Oz*, by Madonna Kolbenschlag. She uses the image of Oz as a metaphor to understand contemporary society. As Dorothy was violently pulled away from home, identity, and community into a strange, alienating place called Oz, in *The Wizard of Oz*, so also are contemporary persons living in Ozlike situations today, alienated from self, intimacy, and community. The underlying alienating forces are male-oriented values that force men and women alike to live false identities, roles that alienate them from their true selves. The most violated in this context are women, constrained to live in a world wherein roles and direction are dictated by male norms. Kolbenschlag calls women especially to a threefold journey: away from Oz to the discovery of the true self; a real at-homeness with the world, rather than the false homes of the culture; and aging, which can be the gradual discovery of true wisdom for life.

Alfred Adler, a former colleague of Freud, and Rudolf Dreikurs, Adler's later disciple, commented on the male/female dichotomy early on in this century. They called the phenomenon *the masculine protest*. The theory of the masculine protest postulates that most men are trying, in Western society, to be "real men." The elusive and illusive problem here is that what constitutes true, healthy masculinity has been poorly defined over the years. The female side of the masculine protest is women clamoring for some of the same privileges and apparent rewards men receive in this male-oriented and dominated society.

More recent studies have focused on a topic related to the masculine protest—that is, the need for a healing of *wounded masculinity* in our time. Spiritual writers like Theodore Dobson have begun to reflect on this issue.

As Adler and Dreikurs put it, most men are striving to become "real men," but have witnessed the significant *absence* of men in the family environment. Men have found their place and security in the work force. Part of Western male socialization has involved the implicit expectation for little boys to separate from their mother's feminine ways by age three or four, to better conform to their father's ways. But then, father is not present or available to mentor or show what it means to be male, or a "real man." The dilemma of our society is boys, as children, teens, and young adults looking for role models on how to be real men in the context of absentee fathers. Dobson feels most contemporary men need real spiritual healing in their relationships with their fathers.

We have been trying to explore the inner landscape of the spiritual journey of adulthood. It is my bias that the critique of Loder, Niebuhr, Gilligan, and the others highlighted in these pages better represent the faith journey of most adults than the neat, clean transitions of the developmentalists. Again, developmentalists probably provide us with language that describes where we at least temporarily arrive in the gradual evolving and unfolding of each adult's vocation and spiritual direction.

St. John the Evangelist, in Streamwood, Illinois, is a parish I serve as weekend associate pastor, and also religious education consultant. St. John's recently held a week-long, traditional mission or retreat, with evening preaching and worship. A novel concept added to the mission was on one day of the mission it was announced that the church would be open one whole day, from morning until early evening, simply for spiritual direction. Those who wanted to come to an open church, to speak with either one of the residential priests, or the religious woman who serves as pastoral associate, were welcomed.

In fact, the three staff members were kept busy the entire day! Streams of persons came all day long to discuss their adulthood, life situations, faith, and to pray with a mentoring figure. Obviously such a small pastoral staff could not afford to spend whole days in spiritual direction with much regularity. But the phenomenon reminded me of the need and hunger for mentoring and spiritual direction among adults, and how, perhaps, this ministry needs to be performed either by small groups, or the nonordained willing to be trained for such a ministry.

Dolores Leckey, a national leader in adult formation, sums up this phenomenon well. Adults, she says, need to learn from adolescents. Adolescents need to "hang around with each other"—and often grow through such "hanging around." Similarly, adults need to learn, says

Leckey, how to waste time, and hang around with each other—helping each other to live, and find God present in their human experience.

There are other developmentalists who have over the last decade and a half studied the dynamics of adult stage transitions from a psycho-social perspective rather than a faith perspective. There is wisdom in their observations too. In fact, the transitions of faith development are set in the context of these states of human development. We turn our attention to their wisdom now.

13

Adult Turning Points

We have already spoken of revelation as God's self-manifestation in ordinary experiences. Similarly, conversion or transformation of life is awakening to that divine presence in the ordinary. We have highlighted how mentoring and community are vital for this experience. Let us now briefly explore the typically human and adult experiences that research has shown to be common to adults—both male and female—in the maturation process. I will synthesize here the pioneering work done by George Vaillant and Daniel Levinson, and their popularizer, Gail Sheehy.

The years 17 to 22 mark for many persons early adult transition. It is characterized as a novicing period in adulthood and adulthood's setting of agenda for work, commitment, and intimacy. It should be noted by pastoral ministers that this age group can be made up of a variety of subpopulations in a faith community: away-from-home college students, commuters or workers, young marrieds, young working singles. The years roughly from 23 to 28 mark the full entering of adulthood. These years witness attempts to create a stable life structure. It should be noted that the twenties begin the adult quest for "the dream" or the idealized life structure, life on the screen of the imagination. During the twenties also people typically seek out *mentoring* figures—if not for the more profound work of finding meaning, as we have already discussed, then at least to receive guidance in the area of career. Though up to ten years ago, 23 to 28 marked the years of entering marriage for most, we are finding commitment to marriage increasingly put off to the late twenties or the thirties. We are witnessing also a tendency to return to home for many during their twenties for economic reasons.

The years 29 to 33 mark the thirties transition. For many, the perceived loss of youth is as difficult to deal with as the mid-life period. Often these years are marked by crisis. It is a natural time for reevaluation of the initial adult life structure. Because of its self-critical, evaluative nature, this period is often marked by divorce, departure from religious life, career change, or some other ritual of radical transition. These can be lonely years for the postdivorce male or female, and "deadline feeling" years for the still single, never married. For those 34 to 40, on the other hand, these are usually settling-down years. But often in the settling-down, there is still discontent, and more of a settling for, than a true settling-down.

For many of those 40 to 45, the mid-life transition begins. Some get through this period with relative ease, but for many the period is characterized by difficult questions about life's meaning, values, and direction. The crisis is often precipitated by the realization that one has lived one-half or more of one's life. Deep questions arise as to whether this is the way one wants to continue living, whether one is self-actualizing, has found true intimacy, is truly happy in job or career. Reappraisal is the name of the game during this period. Levinson and others contend that whether this is truly crisis time or not is often indicated by the degree to which one finds oneself frequently "at odds with" or "over against" superiors, bosses, spouse, family of origin, etc. A high degree of combativeness in one's relationships often indicates the mid-life transition as crisis.

Levinson subdivides mid-life into three categories. The years 45 to 50 are the phase known as "entering middle adulthood." From 50 to 55 is the age 50 transition, and 55 to 60 is the culmination of middle adulthood. The years that make up the now famous era of mid-life are usually a time when males and females feel polarity in their lives. In other words they feel *young and old*—creation *and* destruction going on within them. They feel both masculine *and* feminine. They feel a need to be both attached *and* separate. Mid-lifers also report an exceeding sense of mortality: dealing with both the aging and sickness of parents and early deaths among their peer group creates this consciousness. Among achieving types, this mortality consciousness creates an urgent sense of deadlines. Also among high achievers there is a high incidence of depression, for it is difficult for the "wonder person" to consistently top himself or herself.

The word that Erikson and others have used to characterize the middle years is *generativity.* Mid-lifers are concerned with leaving a mark on succeeding generations. Gilligan finds such a statement too overgeneralizing, for a mother who has given birth to two or three children by age forty certainly is not beginning to get concerned about generativity in her middle years. She has been "generative" since early young adulthood. Not only among the faith-stage developmentalists, but shot through the developmentalists in general, feminists sense a male skewing.

Older adulthood can be characterized by the following categories: 60–65, the late adult transition; 65–80, the senior years; 80 +, the advanced years of old age.

More recent research into the elderly by Irene Burnside (*Working with the Elderly*) speaks of the young old (60–70); the middle-age old (71–80); the old-old (81–90); the very old (91 +).

We will return to some subissues present under the umbrella titles of *mid-life* and *senior years*. But first, let us name some crises or hingelike experiences that seem common to each of the adult stages.

Levinson, Vaillant, and others found certain constants as elements dealt with by adults at each of the stages and substages. They are: an energizing dream, the importance of work, intimacy, mentoring and being mentored, and the process of individuation or becoming one's unique self. Alfred Adler and Rudolf Dreikurs put it another way. They said the "won't go away" issues of life are: self-concept, *Weltanshauung* or worldview, outlook on relationships, moral imperatives, ideals sought after, and the issue of meaning or spirituality. Whichever set of adult issues one chooses to investigate or use, the fact is these constants are the aspects of life around which stage transitions or transformational moments happen or are triggered. Another chapter on adult religious education will look again at the importance of these apparently universal human experiences.

How people weather transition or transformation seems to fall into some rather standard, common tracks. At each stage or substage, some adults:

1. experience genuine growth
2. are themselves stable, but are thrown into a whirlwind because of a serious failure or life accident, not of their own choosing
3. break out of a life situation or structure that is dissatisfying or was a poor choice from the outset
4. experience genuine occupational, fiscal advancements that create problems and impede growth
5. have been in unstable life structures that continue, perhaps even deepen, in patterns of instability

Some Mid-Life Considerations

Janice Brewi and Anne Brennan, in their books *Mid-Life* and *Celebrate Mid-Life,* speak of the middle years as a time when "the Shadow" emerges into consciousness. "The Shadow" is a Jungian term that refers to that which might have been if a dimension of self had been developed, *or* that which one dislikes about the self, or the weak or ugly side of self. The challenge of the middle years is the integration of the Shadow, in fact, in some cases, the transformation of the negative energy of the Shadow into something positive and therapeutic.

Most students of mid-life describe the period as one of pain and existential crisis, but a time in which the pain becomes an opportunity for new wisdom.

Raymond Studzinski, in *Spiritual Direction and Mid-Life Development,* writes that the middle years give one a shifting sense of time. It is also a time for envy and rivalry, especially toward younger generations who seem to enjoy privileges that the mid-lifer lost with aging. It is a deeply spiritual time, when people search for *The Other:* God and intimacy with other human beings.

Though writing specifically for women religious in *Midlife Wanderer—Women Religious in Midlife Transition,* Sheila Murphy hits upon some themes of great significance for all mid-lifers, male or female. Picking up on a notion from Merton, which we touched on in the section on small communities, Murphy highlights the deeply spiritual nature of this period by speaking of it as a time, for many, for a "journey inward." She feels that part of that journey inward involves a period of mourning the obvious losses that are part of mid-life. Mourning includes some rather marked stages of grieving:

—shock and denial
—isolation of the self
—hurt and anger
—panic and feelings of anxiety
—depression and loneliness
—guilt and self-blame around some issues
—gradual emergence of peace, and a sense of reentering the mainstream of life
—a new dignity, determination, and hope

Mid-life is a time also for shifts in experiencing and understanding sexuality. Having peaked in terms of orgasmic ability in the late teens, men begin to understand (or deny) the communication-intimacy connections with physical sexuality. Some women report depression at the death of the womb, or the end of childbearing years. Other women experience a new appreciation of the physical, genital pleasure of sexuality, freed of the concern regarding pregnancy. The "empty nest" syndrome of children leaving home is a welcomed experience by some who rediscover the spousal stranger lost in years of preoccupation with children, or a frightening experience for some couples. For some couples without the flexibility or interest to negotiate around new rules and roles for the relationship, the empty nest can be frightening—often to the point of leading to emotional or legal divorce.

The Aging of the Baby Boomers and New Challenges for Ministry

What will probably be the first of many books and studies of the rapidly growing subpopulation of senior citizens is the *Age Wave* by Ken Dychtwald and Joe Flower. The book speculates on how the current demographic bulge of persons born between 1946 and 1963 will change the shape of American life as it moves first into its middle years, and then its senior years. The basic thrust of *Age Wave* is that never before will so many persons enter senior years in America, never before will we have had so many senior citizens. In the future, to be old will not be looked down on, as it has heretofore, in a youth-worshiping nation. Aging will increasingly be looked on with respect and dignity. Essentially what Dychtwald and Flower are predicting is an end to the phenomenon of agism or negative, cynical, hostile attitudes toward older persons.

The growth of the elderly population is growing faster than that of the nation as a whole. It is projected this growth will continue into the twenty-first century. Since 1965, the 65+ age group has grown by 35 percent while the nation's population as a whole has grown only by 19 percent. By the year 2000 there will be thirty-two million persons age sixty-five and older, 12 percent of the total population. By 2020–2030, three-quarters of health provider time will be spent on older people.

"Normal aging" carries with it some concomitant degeneration, common to most seniors. After age 75, some sensory deficits are experienced by three out of five people. Most experience some hearing loss; a severe degree of this can lead to a paranoid feeling of being cut off from reality. It can become increasingly difficult to trust the world and people. Most experience also deficits in sight, especially in adapting to the dark, making night driving both difficult and dangerous. Decline in smell and taste makes many older persons finicky about their food, or hard to please in restaurants and meals away from home. Aging was described recently at a seminar I attended as "weakness getting stronger."

Besides these rather typical phenomenon, there are more serious problems to be dealt with in some older people. Ten percent of those over 65 have moderate to severe intellectual impairment. Fifteen percent of all seniors over 65 have Alzheimer's Disease—a figure some in the health field consider to be epidemic. Especially for some of these more problematic situations, the National Institute on Aging estimates that there will be an increase in the number of people inhabiting nursing homes, from the current 1.3 million, to 2.1 million in the twenty-first century. Also, among those aged 81 to 90, there are high incidences of depression, organic mental disorders, and chronic disabling diseases. Advancement in medication and technology keeps many more of these people in stable emotional shape, and status quo physical condition.

R. Havighurst, an expert in gerontology, has described the senior years as the "examen years," years that necessitate real analysis of one's life. The examen, or analysis, of necessity includes some discontinuity or life changes. Among the decisions called out for by such analysis are:

—where and how to live remaining years
—how to continue supportive, close relationships with spouse or significant other (this includes the issue of sexual intimacy)
—the need for safe, satisfying living situations
—an adjustment in living standards, parallel with adjustment in financial resources
—how to maintain the maximum level of health
—the need to maintain contact with children, grandchildren, and other relatives
—the maintenance of an interest in human affairs, civic affairs, etc.
—maintenance of old interests, and generation and pursuit of new ones
—the pursuit of meaning in life after retirement

—the working out of a new philosophy of life
—the adjustment required by the death of spouses and other loved ones

What is obvious from Havighurst's list is that ministry to seniors—in both the present and the future—calls out for professionals and ministers deeply interested in and aware of the profound nuances of aging—psychologically, interpersonally, and spiritually. Obviously the "Bingo and Benediction" diet, which most parishes offer the aging, is an insult to the senior years. These years were described by Erik Erikson as years of profound significance, years of recapitulating one's entire lifestyle, discovering either integrity, wholeness, or despair, a feeling of meaninglessness about one's life. A parish ought to become a relational organism that seeks to create an environment that ministers to the whole older person: philosophically, spiritually, physically, socially, and psychologically.

Many ministries could begin for seniors. These ministries might be held on parish campuses, brought to nursing homes, or brought to retirement centers—the increasingly popular kibbutz model for seniors. Ministries might include pastoral care of the sick, social groups, self-help groups; support networks; widows groups; adopt-a-grandchild; babysitting—all with seniors alternatively ministering and being ministered to. Many seniors want to feel they still have something to offer others. Many senior-focused ministries could be done well in *small groups*, not just through one-on-one ministry. The groups could be both *peer-to-peer* and *intergenerational* in nature. In any such effort, seniors' gift of long-term memory and story can be employed to enrich their peers, as well as other age groups. As parishes seek to edge seniors toward integrity, seniors in turn have much wisdom to offer the rest of the community.

Ministering to those Parenting their Parents and to Parents of Mid-Life Children: The Four-Generation Family

A woman on a radio talk show said it well recently: "I never knew being in mid-life would be so difficult. I have to care for my children, my grandchildren, my parents, and my husband, and myself. *Myself* would be quite enough at this point." The woman was voicing the angst and struggle of many in their forties and fifties. Perhaps the most complex phenomenon the woman spoke of was having to care for one's parents. In a subsequent chapter, I will speak of the responsibility of the parochial school or conventional catechetical programs to not just service children, but rather to make part of its curriculum a ministry to family life, helping parents to better relate to their children, and children to their parents. We will speak later about the urgency parishes ought to feel about helping to create the domestic, household church.

We close off consideration of adult development with the admonition that parishes help that large group of baby-boomers spoken of earlier to better relate to their senior citizen parents. It is the same principle articulated in the previous paragraph, applied to a different end of the age spectrum. Parishes would do well to help mid-lifers relate to seniors, and in turn seniors to their mid-life children.

If there is loss to be mourned in the middle years, that certainly is the case in the senior years. Part of ministry to seniors is helping them name and mourn their losses. Part of ministry is helping the mid-life child to understand the inner world of the senior citizen, and the senior citizen to understand the never experienced before stress-level of the typical mid-lifer. What I am suggesting here is similar to parent and teacher effec-tiveness training seminars; I am suggesting communication training. So much "bad air" between seniors and mid-lifers boils down to missed or misinterpreted communication. The parish of the future has to advocate bridge-building between parents and teenage children. And there is another chasm to bridge, that between adult children and their parents.

Between these two groups, some of the same issues that exist between mid-life parents and teens can exist: communication, roles, rules, power, control. In their book, *Surviving Your Aging Parents* by Bernard Shulman and Raeann Berman describe four types of relationships that can exist between adult children and their parents.

1. *status equality:* in this relational style, senior and mid-life approach each other as two adults with equal status.

2. *status quo:* in this scenario, older parents hold sway, in a lopsided way, over their mid-life children; nothing essentially has changed in terms of the parents' control over their adult children, though both have aged physically.

3. *status conflict:* this is a combative-type relationship, in which the elderly parent feels power and control are being taken from him or her;

usually the senior has not been prepared for this, and therefore is unwilling to relinquish the trappings of power, control, and self-determination.

4. *status reversal:* in this case, weakened parents have to relinquish autonomy and depend upon their adult children; in effect dominion is relinquished.

Often older people locked in the conflict of (3) above are in *need* of status reversal. The conflict arises because authority is being taken from them rather than being renegotiated in a spirit of collaboration.

I do not intend to favor, in this section, the senior citizen. The mid-life child is certainly in need of guidance and ministry. The new world of caring for an aging parent is a world with no rules, a world in which many of us need to feel our way, grope along, never knowing exactly how much or how little to do. Often one child among siblings becomes a caretaker figure, handling more of the responsibility for the family than the other adult children. Communication problems and bad feelings can crop up among brothers and sisters.

Again the importance of groups, age segregated, intergenerational and family-based communities—a smorgasbord experience of small communities—in addition to other ministries seem to hold the key to better ministry in this area in the future. Perhaps not until now have family oriented pastoral ministers understood how loaded the terms *parent,* and *parenting* would become.

14
Andragogy—Adult Learning Praxis

In 1985 Dolores Leckey addressed the Adult Ministries Consultation, held at the Cardinal Spellman Retreat Center in the Bronx, New York. Her theme was adult Christian faith. In her excellent address, she highlighted six themes she associates with maturing adult Christian faith. They are:

1. *The open way.* Adult faith is very much a journey, a pilgrimage. Leckey's metaphor sums up the experience and research of previous chapters of this book.

2. *Heightened vocation.* Part of the adult journey is hearing and responding to the call of God in the depths of one's life—calling each of us to a unique direction. Vocation is something we all have. With aging it takes on different shapes and sizes.

3. *Inclusiveness.* Adult faith is expansive, taking in and seeking meaning in and for more and more of human experience.

4. *Suffering and loss.* We saw over and over again, in the classical and more current theories of human development, that conversion often involves pain—or as Boff would put it, God's reign breaks in through our poverty.

5. *Childlike play.* Most healthy adults discover or rediscover their *child*, that part of each of us that is still able to be struck by wonder, enjoy recreation, and the regeneration that comes with nonproductivity.

6. *Gratitude.* One of the chief signs of a truly converting heart is a life lived in an ongoing posture of praise.

Leckey's six themes poetically sum up so much of what we have discussed in the two previous chapters. She is reechoing one of the chief biases of this book, that conversion—transformation—is gradually evolving and unfolding in the ordinary experience of human life.

It is the responsibility of religious education, religious educators, to help, to facilitate this "awakening to revelation" experience.

In 1985 the United States Catholic Conference issued a document entitled *Serving Life and Faith: Adult Religious Education and the American Catholic Community.* The document, though several years old now, has remained an important one for me, for it stated authoritatively a constant I have held to in seventeen years at adult faith-formation. For people to experience revelation in their ordinary experience, their parishes need to offer quality adult education processes that help them find and name God in the ordinary. I emphasize the core message of this document, because I fear quality needs-based, needs-responded-to adult religious education, based on study of a local parish or cluster of parishes, has been replaced by the prepackaged, multimedia programs produced by other people, of another place, perhaps superficially acquainting people with current church thought or scripture study, but not helping them to meet God in their own vulnerability and humanity.

Serving Life and Faith says that the ministry of adult religious education is a major part of the parish's overall responsibility for the ministry of the word. The document articulates three goals for adult religious education: to attempt to help adults live the gospel; to help adults become prophetic voices in the world; and to help adults pass on faith to succeeding generations. The document states that the ideal of adult education is contemporary believers taking on the posture of the disciples in Acts 2, in the Pentecostal experience of church. Such adult believers would be "devoted to . . . instruction and the communal life . . . going to the Temple . . . gathering in homes for the Breaking of the Bread . . . and devoted to prayer . . . sharing all in common . . . based on needs. Adult religious education facilitates ongoing learning and transformation opportunities, fosters community, is Eucharist focused, is rooted in prayer, and oriented toward the transformation of society, social justice." We hear reechoed here the staples of small community and faith formation.

Adult religious education, the document says, is ministry to and toward discipleship. In trying to develop disciples, adult religious educators need to be realistic and patient. Many middle-class Catholics and Protestants would resist being discipled. Tough, well meaning and intentioned, their hearts are wedded to consumer capitalistic values. An effective adult religious educator will be resisted by many in the middle class. He or she may also find one's self in tension with the trappings of institutionalized bureaucratic churches. As Allan Figueroa Deck points out in his book on the evangelization of Hispanic immigrants, *The Second Wave,* often what is most needed in America is not the evangelization of the given individual immigrant, but rather the evangelization by the immigrant of secular and ecclesial cultures that are counter-gospel.

When we hear words like adult *religious education* or *instruction,* we immediately jump to *lecture,* classroom-type connotations. That is because many still connect adult religious education with either overchurchy programs of tradition passing or *pedagogy,* which is how we teach children. Be assured, in this advocacy for adult religious education I am advocating neither. We need no more churchy programs that attract churchy people. We need opportunities that appeal to and touch real needs felt and experienced by adults. In such opportunities skilled facilitators can help ordinary adults make the jump from the area of human needs to the spiritual dimension indwelling the human need. Leon McKenzie in *The Religious Education of Adults* speaks of the adult as a coordinated system of intellect, feelings, somatic experiences, morality, relationships, and so on. In quality adult religious education, a bearing down on a need in any one piece of the system can lead to a discovery of the God of mystery present in questions, needs, and humanity.

Let me reiterate, in addition to not being over theological and churchy, neither is quality adult religious education heavily cerebral or typically academic in nature. Such a learning model is what Malcolm Knowles, Leon McKenzie, Nancy Foltz, Paulo Freire, Thomas Groome, and others have helped us to see, over the years, to be pedagogy, or teaching methods for children. Pedagogy presumes someone will volitionally come to a learning experience, assimilate material someone else has told him or her is important, store the information for later use—usually to pass an examination. For good or for ill, that is how many elementary school-age children are still made to learn. But adults resist that type of learning; only the most "churchy" will come to that type of learning. Adults are practical learners. They come, with healthy self-interest, to experiences that help them live.

The person in America credited with discovering this is Malcolm Knowles, whose ideals can be found in *The Modern Practice of Adult Education; From Pedagogy to Andragogy. Pedagogy* refers to child learning praxis, *andragogy* to adult learning praxis. The roots for both words are in the Greek words of child *(paidos)* and adult *(andros).* While Knowles approached andragogy from a secular perspective, Paulo Freire has adapted similar principles for spiritual formation and political action. Leon

McKenzie, Nancy Foltz, and Thomas Groome have adapted similar principles for religious education. Let us briefly examine the principles of andragogy, stripped of theology and spirituality in the manner of Malcolm Knowles.

In contrast to the information-storing kind of learning, characteristic of pedagogical methods of learning, andragogy operates out of a different set of principles. Malcolm Knowles systematized these principles only after years of observing that late adolescents, young adults, and adults seemed to learn and grow the most with teachers who were informal in manner and student-centered, rather than curriculum-preoccupied in their approach to education. Knowles finally articulated a set of convictions, based on his andragogical foundation:

1. Adult learners are or ought to become self-directing.

2. Adults bring into any learning situation a wealth of experience, which contains much insight and wisdom.

3. Adults come to learning experiences when motivated by a need in their life, to improve the quality of their lives, or to solve problems.

4. Thus, adult orientation to learning is life-centered, task-centered, or problem-centered.

5. The most potent motivators to learning experiences for adults are growth in self-esteem, recognition by significant others, a better quality of life, greater self-actualization, greater self-confidence, and other qualitative aspects of life.

Unlike pedagogy, in which some expert determines, or ascribes, both needs and program design to waiting learners, andragogy involves a multistep process.

1. Climate setting. Classroom settings are the least helpful and appealing to adults, the least conducive to learning. In most instances, the more relaxed, physically comfortable climate present in many *small Christian communities* would seem to be more the ideal than lecture-type settings.

In addition to physical climate, there is also psychological climate. Knowles felt that a healthy psychological climate involves mutual respect among members; collaboration; mutual trust and support; humanness, openness, and authenticity with each other; and pleasure.

2. Participants join together in diagnosing of their own life needs.

3. Participants are involved in setting the goals and objectives to be learned.

4. Participants, with assistance, design a plan and process for growth and learning.

5. Leaders help learners in carrying out their learning plans.

6. Leaders and learners collaborate in evaluation and planning for the future.

Over the years Knowles retitled his book, from *The Modern Practice of Adult Education: Pedagogy vs. Andragogy* to *The Modern Practice of Adult Education: From Pedagogy to Andragogy.* He made the change to indicate that the two styles of formation and learning are not antithetical to each other, but on a continuum. Some adults indeed may need a pedagogical style before growing into or being comfortable with an andragogical style.

An andragogical approach would not simply assess nonattendance or nonparticipation as "failure." Poor attendance is often symptomatic—that something was not done well enough in the andragogical process. A frequent transgression is for adult religious educators to *ascribe* needs to parishioners, rather than listen to needs and then do planning. Another transgression is to impose one style of learning or impose one style on divergent personality types, rather than offer a variety of learning techniques based on asking adults what they like, want, or need.

I am frequently asked to help parishes or dioceses to design adult religious education processes. I am rather persistent in at least some principles of andragogy: the importance of beginning with need-discernment of the worshiping community; the importance of widening need-discernment to include the marginally involved through home visitation; the necessity of questioning parishioners about convenient times; and formats that truly facilitate. The results of such surveying often reveal concerns like: How do I parent better? How do I improve my marriage? How do you make a moral decision today? How do I cope with stress, depression, and anxiety?

The immediate concerns of the professional religious educator might be much more theological and ecclesial. For the ordinary believer—active or inactive in participation—the concerns are more immediate and human. Addressing some of these apparently preevangelical needs through gospel filters can help people move into the more obviously spiritual, mysterious dimensions of life. Good adult religious education can be a very effective way of reaching out to the so-called alienated Catholic.

Andragogy is a vital approach in facilitating the relational, intellectual, behavioral, imaginative faith spoken of in a previous chapter. The best examples of andragogy are frequently found in *RCIA processes and small Christian communities.*

Part III

Family Consciousness

15

The Domestic Church and a Family Perspective

For years, the master teacher and catechist Johannes Hofinger lamented the state of religious education in the United States. His critique was twofold: sacraments were distributed or celebrated with no concern for perceived conversion; religious education efforts seemed too focused on children, to the exclusion of parental involvement. We return to the old metaphors for parish life—school, CCD, and organizations, with the first two excessively preoccupied with children. *Will Our Children Have Faith?* asks John Westerhoff in his book of the same title. His answer is *no,* not if we stay wedded to child-centered catechesis that sidelines mother and father. Remember one of George Gallup's recent suggestions to improve evangelization in the mainline churches—stop educating children and start evangelizing families.

Offical ecclesial concern about the family was articulated in 1978, when the United States Bishops' Conference published its *Plan of Pastoral Action for Family Ministry.* In it, the bishops called for a renewed mission of enhancing the church's awareness of the sacramental nature of marriage, enabling couples and families to care for each other, establishing peer ministers for marriage and family life, and establishing structures that facilitate these ideals.

The bishops' statement was followed by Pope John Paul's encyclical *Familiaris Consortio.* In this letter, the pope pushed the notion of base community to its extreme. Families, he said, are the basic unit of church; they are the domestic church. In fact, he said, the future of evangelization largely depends on the evangelizing activity of the family. In addition to being the basic cell of church, families are also the basic nurturing forces of society as a whole. The pope agreed that certain specific, unique

115

ministries are needed for the family; but he added that the *family* needs not just another spate of ministries but must become rather the *lens* through which other pastoral activities are viewed and experienced.

No one would disagree with the ideals set forth by either the bishops or the pope, yet those ideals must be seen up against some problematic facts.

The Family under Seige

The National Catholic Education Association released the following information recently:

—Only 10 percent of American families live in what we used to look on as the typical arrangement of two live-in parents and children.

—Forty percent of mothers with infants must work; 70 percent of mothers with children of school-age must work. Children rarely experience a stay-at-home parent.

—Though the surge has leveled off in the last ten years or so, divorce has increased 700 percent since the turn of the century. This steady rise really began around the time of the Civil War.

—Half of first marriages end in divorce; 60 percent of second marriages end in divorce. Catholic statistics are congruent with those of the rest of the nation. This phenomenon has given birth to two other struggles: single parenting and blended families.

—The number of couples living together without marriage rose 157 percent from 1970 to 1980.

—One out of every five babies is born out of wedlock, an increase of 50 percent over a decade ago.

—We are witnessing in America the feminization of poverty. Female heads of families have poverty rates six times those of two-parent families.

—The top 5 percent of American families own 43 percent of the net wealth in the nation; while the bottom 50 percent of American families hold 4 percent of the nation's net wealth.

—In terms of mobility, 50 percent of all Americans changed residence between 1975 and 1980.

—Marriages increasingly are beginning later and fostering fewer children.

—Nearly half of all children in the United States currently will live with *one parent* before they finish high school.

—By 1990 the combined total of single-parent and blended households will be larger than the total of never-divorced two-parent families.

—Not bad news, but to be noted is the following: Hispanics comprise 25 percent of the Catholic Church in the United States. African Americans are increasingly taking advantage of Catholic parish and school services. Immigration of Catholic Asians is on the rise.

—The bad news in the Hispanic–African American–Asian phenomenon is the insensitivity that parishes often display toward the plight and culture of the stranger, the recent immigrant. Though many of the Hispanics and Asians especially may consider themselves culturally Catholic, they are more and more seduced by evangelical proselytizers.

All the above suggests that the vision of family life is confused in the United States. In the recent decades we have moved from a familial-communitarian society to technological-individualistic society. Society pays more attention to individuals than to the social context, the social system of family. As a society, we have not caught up—especially in terms of aid and services—to the complexities inherent in family life today.

What has been talked about in church circles for some years now, and has finally been articulated clearly, is the notion of *a family perspective*. The document recently published on this topic by the U.S. bishops is entitled *A Family Perspective in Church and Society*. Before getting to a description of a family perspective, let us further underscore the reason for advocating such a view. Family functions are now being shared with other groups and institutions; many basic family functions are now overreliant on professionals. Most of these "professionals" focus on individuals and not the family, or social context of which the individual is a part. Some family functions are being totally taken over by nonfamily, professional outsiders.

A family perspective is an attitudinal (leading to behavioral) attempt to break down our society's preoccupation with the individual, to view the individual in his or her *social context,* and to minister not just to the individual but also to the social context. Advocates of a family perspective prophetically say that the parish, the church as a whole, mirrors consumer society in how we do ministries and programs. As society focuses on the individual, so also do many of our ministerial efforts. A family perspective consistently sees beyond the individual to a person's network of social systems: society as a whole, institutions, groups, and the family. The *family* and other social networks become, in a family perspective, the lens through which we plan and evaluate programs and ministries.

Family Impact Questions

One simple means to begin implementing a family perspective is, in futuring or evaluation of a program already completed, to ask questions that assess the impact of the given ministry on an individual's social context. Some examples of such *family impact* questions are:

—Does this program address just the individual, the individual in relation to his or her family, or the overall needs of the entire family?

—Are there any members of a family deliberately excluded by a program or ministry (e.g., a noncustodial parent)? If so, how could such people be included?

—Is the program or ministry too much directed toward one socio-economic group? For example, is an overnight retreat possible for some of the teens in a parish, but cost-prohibitive for others? Could the choice of place or style of the retreat be altered to become more socio-economically inclusive?

—Is there built into a ministry a process that helps families deal with the changes the ministry or program might cause in the individual and therefore also the social context in which he/she lives? Are we ready, for example, to help families reassimilate individuals who have been through the RCIA? An overnight retreat?

—Are families involved in program planning, implementation, and evaluation? This simply is an extension of the principles of andragogy discussed in a previous chapter.

Relationship with Society

A family perspective, then, is an attitude of advocacy *within the church itself,* encouraging ministers, ministries, programs to use family, social context as a *lens,* for planning and evaluation. But a family perspective also involves the church, serving as an advocate for the family to and in society itself. This necessitates parishes breaking out of the "city of God enclave," ecclesiology we discussed earlier, wherein we look at ourselves, parishes, church, as alternatives to the world. Rather than retreating from the world, we as church, in fact, enter into dialogue with the world and its institutions—schools, hospitals, clinics, psychotherapy centers, social-recreational facilities, local governments, etc.—advocating the rights and needs of families, entering into partnership with these bodies in serving the family. Also relative to society, ministry via a family perspective teaches families to become more assertive and aggressive in claiming and reclaiming their rights and responsibilities relative to church and society.

A Family Perspective in Church and Society

Published in 1987, this episcopal statement on a family perspective says that such a perspective seeks to propagate a *Christian* vision of family life. The document describes the family as an intimate community of persons *bonded* by blood, marriage, adoption, or choice. This intimate community serves life and is a natural base comunity for social training. It also is in dialogue with God, and, as a small cell, shares in the total evangelical mission of the church.

The document also says that a parish implementing a family perspective:

—views the family as a developing system, helps the family to understand itself as in flux, and provides different ministries for and to the different stages of family life;

—is aware of and ministers to the family diversity present in families today (remember the absence of "the traditional arrangement" discussed earlier);

—and advocates healthy, life-serving partnership between families and other institutions.

The document on family perspective reminds us that what is needed in the future are family-sensitive ministers who will advocate the vision articulated here, create specific family ministries, sponsor family forums and activities, encourage family-based catechesis, and facilitate pastoral counseling opportunities for families.

A Model for Implementing a Family Perspective

Father J. Daryl Furlong directs the Office of Family Ministry in Madison, Wisconsin. His research, along with that of his staff, have led to the production of an exciting vision and praxis for implementing both a family perspective and the principles of andragogy. In 1987 Buckley

Publications of Chicago published a synthesis of the Madison strategies in book-form, *The Ministry of Listening: Ministering with a Family Perspective*. Furlong says that at the heart of ministry with a family perspective is listening. Ministers to families need to listen. A parish would benefit from the development of a family ministry team that enters into formation and training to prepare them for *formal listening*—listening to families and to individuals that make up families. The basic tool for listening is a family inventory or survey, administered in different ways (e.g., at liturgy, in special groupings, through home visits) to different age groups. Efforts are made to listen to people who are truly representative of the entire parish. The inventory seeks to name who is in the parish in terms of demographics (married, single, young adult, senior citizen, etc.), and the needs of the various demographic groups—basic human needs the parish can help with, as well as obviously spiritual needs.

After a summary report of all this information is compiled, then the family ministry team, working with the staff, proposes processes and structures that will facilitate ministries and programs that address the articulated needs of families. Special attention is given also to the needs of children and teens, and ministries that they may need.

The ministry of listening is an effective means of making a family perspective workable. We turn now to three areas of concentration in better evangelizing and ministering to family life: supportive ministries to marriage, ministry to parents, and family-based models of religious education.

16

Growing Married

Andrew Greeley has said through the years that perhaps we invest too much time and money at the wrong end of marriage. We mandate, in most dioceses, premarital preparation; but over the years of my priesthood, I have seen precious little in the area of ongoing marriage enrichment. At the parishes where I have served these past sixteen years, I have tried to initiate or contribute to two ongoing ministries: marriage preparation and ongoing marriage enrichment. In this chapter we will focus on the need for the latter.

Getting vs. Growing Married

In both marriage preparation and enrichment, I try to get couples to "clean up their language." When a man and woman speak of their marriage in the church, they speak of "getting married." That notion of "getting married" is simply reflective of the language we use for all of our sacraments. We *"get baptized, absolved, ordained, anointed, communion, confirmed."* Our language of *getting* betrays a *reification* or *thingification* of sacrament. Actually sacraments are ritual celebrations, steps in a process of growth. Each of the seven sacred rituals ought to have an existential growth process that leads up to the celebration, and a new life stance that flows from the celebration.

Specifically, for our discussion of marriage, one simply cannot *get married*. Two persons can *grow married, become married,* or *become divorced* (or, I suppose, *remain stagnant*). The sacramental ritual is a step in a process. Neither should a couple be encouraged to *stay* married; for that is the language of *survival,* or sticking it out with each other. Again, the goal is to engage in the mystery of *becoming married.*

121

From Contract to Friendship

Sacramental marriage, the mystery of two becoming one, is truly a counter-cultural movement and statement. Sound catechesis is needed in preparation for and throughout the course of living the sacrament. Four images that I think are important to share with couples regarding matrimony are:

1. *Contract.* Civil law speaks of marriage as a contract. Though this is the minimal interpretation of the meaning of marriage, there are elements inherent in the image of contract that are helpful for understanding Christian marriage. A contract is an agreement between two or more people. For two people or organizations to grow in a contractual relationship, there needs to be, over the years, effective negotiation and renegotiation. *Becoming married,* on just the contractual level, demands ongoing conversation about roles, rules, and expectations—all of which shift and require reinterpretation over months and years.

2. *Covenant.* This image is borrowed from the Old Testament period. The Jewish people gradually came to understand their bond with God as a covenant, or an unbreakable bond. Eventually they came to apply this image to their marriages: as Yahweh was in an unbreakable bond with them, so they were challenged to be faithful in love with and for each other. This image has become important in Christian writing about marriage. It speaks well of the ideals of fidelity and indissolubility inherent in Christian marriage.

3. *Sacrament.* St. Augustine was among the first to stress the sacramentality of marriage. In Catholic tradition, marriage as sacrament has at least two connotations: (a) *sign.* Marriage is a sign of a deeper, more profound, reality: God's covenant with the people. A sacramental couple mirrors or signs to the world God's unconditional love as they try to unconditionally love each other. (b) *vow.* As we stated in an earlier chapter, Tertullian, who predated Augustine, interpreted the word *sacramentum* in the old Roman sense of *vow.* In sacramental vowing, a person gives one's heart, one's living, dying, and rising to the Lord and to the community in which the Spirit abides. In marriage, a couple *vow* to each other to be for and with each other forever. Notice the *ecclesiology* emerging in this theology of marriage. The small community of matrimony is embedded in the communitarian experience of the Trinity and the body of Christ, the church.

4. *Friendship.* In the fifteenth chapter of John's Gospel, Jesus tries to explain the nature of the friendship he has developed with his apostles. He says: "The greatest love a man can have for his friends is to give his life for

them. And you are my friends, if you do what I command you. I do not call you servants any longer, because a servant does not know what his master is doing. Instead, I call you friends, because I have told you everything I heard from my Father. You did not choose me; I choose you, and appointed you to go and bear much fruit, the kind of fruit that endures. . . . The Father will give you whatever you ask of Him in my name. This, then, is what I command you: love one another."

Key elements of Jesus' description of friendship can be applied to the kind of friendship a marriage ideally should become.

—*Lay down one's life.* Marital friendship has to transcend the measuring approach of conditional love—that is, the "I'll give if you give" approach. To be willing to lay down one's life is to leave go of all game-playing, and to be willing to give even if one is not given to.

—*I do not speak of you as servants (slaves).* It is so easy for any relationship, including marriage, to degenerate into a master-slave relationship, or one in which one party is superior and the other is inferior, one is in charge and the other is not. The only healthy relationship, including marriage, is one in which both parties approach each other as equal.

—*I have told you everything.* In saying that he has shared what the Father has revealed to him, Jesus is equivalently saying that he has shared the core of his inner world with his friends. This also is a quest for marital friendship, to share inner worlds with each other. Marital friendship is more than collaboration: it is communication of feelings and thoughts that leads to communion with each other.

—*I chose you.* Married love involves more than emotions. Married friends love each other when they feel like it and when they do not feel like it. Love, while involving emotion and passion, is essentially a decision for another.

—*Go and bear fruit.* True friends, especially married friends, make life better for each other. Married life needs to be more than survival or coping. Married partners genuinely enrich the lives of each other.

—*Ask the Father in my name.* We need to ground all our relationships in prayer. Married partners qualitatively change their relationships when they pray with each other and for each other each day.

Beyond Genitality to Sexuality

The sexual revolution has changed the thinking of many people in our culture. The media seem to almost set the criteria for what healthy sexual expression and morality look like. Young people are becoming sexually active earlier and earlier in the developmental process. Estimates are that up to one-third of the American husbands have been unfaithful to their wives at some point in their relationship. The importance of genital sexual expression is proclaimed "evangelistically" in movies, TV shows, rock music, and music videos.

Perhaps genital expression is more important than the church has previously indicated, but it is only one part of the larger fabric of marriage, and communication in a marriage. Sexuality is a broad notion that includes physical touch but also communication, emotional sharing, and each partner's feelings about self as a male or female. Couples need to reach for a healthy sexual life, in a holistic sense, rather than narrowing their shared vision to focus on genital acts. Genital acts indeed need to be talked about, with each partner being open and honest about needs, likes and dislikes, and with each partner really striving to please his/her partner. Human sexuality is one of life's beautiful gifts in which two people can experience interpersonal communion.

Predictable Stages

Dr. Eugene Kennedy and others have spoken of both the individual and relational stages people go through who are married to each other. Kennedy feels that if people practiced greater understanding toward their partner's stage, or both had greater patience with a stage that the relationship was going through, there probably would be fewer divorces in America.

Cynthia Smith writes on some of the predictable stages of a marriage in her book *The Seven Levels of Marriage.* She begins the book by addressing the area of expectations. What each partner expects and demands of each other is something that necessitates ongoing mutual accommodation and compromise. Accommodation and compromise are, she says, the "language of love." I like to put it another way: true love is like a reed that bends with the wind. An immature or nonintegral love is like a brittle branch that is snapped or broken by the wind, until it no longer is a reality. Smith's seven stages are as follows:

1. *The entry period.* Two persons have to learn to relate to the reality of his/her partner, rather than the ideal; at this stage both partners can be "hedging" on commitment to each other.

2. *The acceptance stage.* Trust grows, and there is a mutual commitment to the relationship; the scoreboard is thrown away.

3. *Parenthood.* In contemporary society, the decision for or against children is much more of a weighty decision than it was in previous years; couples are consciously deciding about the time for and number of children, or if there will be children at all.

4. *Family stage.* Becoming a family radically changes the time and energy the couple have for each other. Caution is needed here to insure quality time, lest "uncoupling" begin. The male often feels jealousy at this stage toward the attention given by the wife to the children and not him. Economics become a greater concern.

5. *The mid-life stage.* This stage is often a "rebirth" time for the woman who can at least partially begin a new leg of life's journey as the responsibilities of mothering change. It is a time for reconciliation for the male, who must come to terms with inevitable career limitations, and the death of some dreams of success and accomplishment.

6. *The hum-drum stage.* Often a part of the mid-life stage, this is a time when boredom sets into a relationships. Hard work is required at this stage on the part of both partners to counter the possibilities of "affairs." A man can become preoccupied with reclaiming his youth in an attempt to deny mortality; on both parts, there can be a return to me-ism.

7. *Freedom.* The senior years, in a sound marriage, can be the experience of "back to just us," freedom from excessive responsibilities, a new sexual intimacy; it also can involve the conflicts of dealing with each other full-time, twenty-four hours a day, and coping with sickness and death.

Dolores Curran in her articles and books articulates stages of married life similar to Smith's stages.

A Spiritual View of the Process

A growing marriage might be diagramed as in Figure 5.

Both partners retain their individuality but work at becoming a couple, with shared values, priorities, and spirituality. Speaking from a Christian perspective, the resurrection of becoming a "we" involves a great deal of dying on both sides, to expectations, resentments, traditions, roles, and individually declared rules for the relationship. A growing marriage is a death and resurrection process over and over again, a process of healing and reconciliation. Such a marriage can genuinely become a marriage in the

Figure 5: Two *Is* Evolve into a *We*

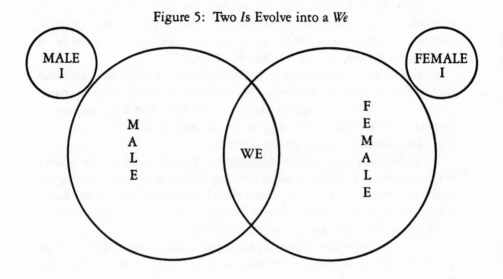

Lord, wherein a couple mutually ministers to each other, tries to transform their home into a little "domestic church" where the values and presence of Jesus are experienced, and where the family in small ways realizes its mission to make a contribution to the society around it. A real challenge in this model is to retain a healthy sense of self and individuation in the process of becoming one, thus avoiding the toxic situation of unhealthy, overdependent enmeshment with each other.

Uncoupling

Retired Judge William Keene now presides daily on the television show *Divorce Court*. He was quoted recently in a newspaper as to what he feels leads most people to divorce courts. Why do one out of every two marriages end in divorce? He replied that the process of divorce starts when communication stops between people. By communication, Keene cautions, he means all kinds—verbal, sexual, emotional, and financial. When one or more of these types of communication is missing, other problems already present and perhaps not attended to become exacerbated and aggravated.

It is important to note Keene's expansive notion of communication. A priest was challenged at a recent parish council meeting for not communicating enough with people in the bulletin. He protested that he did clearly announce decisions and events in the bulletin and from the pulpit. Some very honest parishioners gently reminded the pastor that true communication was not just the passing of information but rather necessitated more a give and take, emotional sharing, participation in decision-making, and getting to know each other.

Diane Vaughn, in a recent book, *Uncoupling,* documents some of the stages of erosion that a relationship goes through when communication breaks down. She uses the metaphor of cars in a train "uncoupling" as an image of what this process looks like. In a dying relationship, partners *first of all* find alternative sources of enjoyment, relaxation, and support. These often are hobbies, belonging to clubs, organizations, more time at work, etc. A *second phase* may include one or both parties sending off signals of discontent with the relationship. If the couple is fortunate these signals are sent clearly and directly. If not, they are often missed, ignored, not perceived. This leads to *a third stage* of seeking out new confidants, new relationships, perhaps transitional figures, perhaps more permanent relationships, who fill the relational void. With a growing sense of distance from one's partner, one begins to *socialize and "scout the territory"* for a new possible future. The relationship by this stage is often in such disrepair that it may lead to one or both parties initiating a *confrontation* about the future of the relationship. This confrontation may lead to a period of *trying,* or therapeutic activity, which may or may not be successful—based on the degree of erosion in the relationship. Often the trying stage is strategically too late, and it unfolds into the *final stage of uncoupling*— emotional and usually legal divorce. Some emotionally divorced people stay with each other, without going through the additional stage of legal divorce.

Emotional divorce, put more concisely, involves *disenchantment* with each other, which is a normal, in fact healthy, part of most relationships as people begin to see each other in less idealized, more realistic ways; *erosion,* which is a negative turn after disenchantment rather than a turn toward learning and improvement; *detachment,* which Rhett Butler describes beautifully to Scarlett O'Hara in *Gone With the Wind:* "Frankly my dear, I don't give a damn!" It is hard to resuscitate a marriage at the detachment stage. All of this leads to emotional divorce, or the emotional death of a relationship.

Central Issues in Marriage Enrichment

Whether in a parish mission format for married couples, or ongoing marriage enrichment series, or premarriage preparation, I share the following issues with couples as central for growing married. I explain them under the umbrella titles "Toxins to be Checked" and "Therapeutic Attitudes and Behaviors to Practice." I present these as recurring issues I deal with as a psychotherapist at a secular mental health facility, as well as a pastoral psychotherapist for parishes in the archdiocese of Chicago.

Toxins to Be Checked

1. *Expectations.* Sometimes the *expectations* couples put on each other are not articulated clearly. A spouse expects the other "to know." Also, often expectations are impossible or unreasonable—beyond the giftedness or ability of the partner to adequately respond. Sometimes the person who has to change relative to expectations is the *self.*

2. *Emotional Divorce.* Earlier we described two flow charts as to what emotional divorce feels like. A couple always needs to be observing whether such deterioration is setting in. Early intervention is vital.

3. *Not Waiting for Each Other.* Again, with Dr. Kennedy, I urge couples to *wait* for each other. The stance of the 1960s, 70s, and 80s—if the relationship is not immediately gratifying, get rid of it—has not proven to be effective, helpful wisdom.

4. *Unresolved Issues from the Past.* Spouses can bring baggage from the past with them into a present relationship. Each individual needs to scrutinize whether he or she is bringing toxins from one's family of origin into a current relationship, and in effect is dynamiting the current relationship.

5. *Realistic Unmet Needs.* Related to the expectations issue, there can be real-life, reasonable needs one or both parties have that are swept under the rug. Couples need to practice the courage to communicate.

6. *Passive Aggression.* Silence, avoidance behaviors, a resistance to talk and share can be more destructive at times than active aggression.

7. *Blame/Counter Blame.* This dynamic becomes like a game of volleyball, until one or both sides stop "passing the ball" and own responsibility for some of the problems in the relationship.

8. *Communication.* Erich Fromm described communication as sharing from the very center of one's self—whether the feelings be warm and fuzzy, or dark and angry. What matters, said Fromm, is that two people practice sharing from the center of their being. Many people who were trained to moralize or judge their feelings are reluctant to articulate what they consider "bad feelings."

9. *Female/Male Differences.* Often we forget the message of Carol Gilligan and others that men and women have been socialized into different internal worlds. Patient understanding of and empathy toward each other's internal worlds are vital.

10. *Power Struggles.* The greatest enemy to love, says sociologist Tony Campolo, is power. The power-broking person is usually the least capable of love, whereas the person not in need of power usually has the greatest capacity to love. Jesus on the cross is the best reminder of what nonpower-seeking, sacrificial love is like.

Therapeutic Attitudes and Behaviors to Practice

1. *Willingness to change self.* AA and other 12-step programs have taught us the uselessness of trying to make someone else over, and the need we all have to better modulate our own behavior and emotional responses to things.

2. *Expressed caring.* Couples ought not to presume that the significant other knows he or she is loved; that love ought to be incarnated, enfleshed regularly, in word and deed.

3. *Encouragement.* We all know what is wrong with us. We need to hear about what is good, beautiful. In a discouraging world of work and societal ills, couples ought to take deliberate steps at encouraging each other. Note that encouragement is not phoney praise, but rather helping another discover his or her goodness, gifts, and beauty.

4. *Learning to confront but not put down.* In sweeping unmet needs under the rug, the bump under the rug can become a mountain that explodes into an insurmountable mountain. On a regular basis, nonpejorative confrontations, that are not demeaning but honest, ought to be practiced.

5. *Sharing decision-making—shaping and changing.* With the stages of a happy marriage and family, a key to happy marriages and parenting is the flexibility to change how rules and decisions are made as the relational system shifts.

6. *Conflict resolution.* Some avoid conflict. Others always have to win. Healthy couples work at facing conflict and resolving it, in a win-win type of strategy with both partners mutually satisfied.

7. *Change "stinkin' thinkin'."* When spouses think or talk negatively about each other, using adverbs *always* and *never,* they have begun to stereotype each other, thus locking the other in a kind of nongrowth prison.

8. *Time.* Without deliberate attention to a relationship, a relationship will get away from us. In conventional marriages, everything gets time *but* the marital relationship. I encourage married couples to date each other regularly, and on a daily basis have at least twenty to thirty minutes of alone time to talk.

9. *Learn communication.* We could all benefit from striving for Fromm's ideals about communication.

10. *Healing prayer.* When Jesus instructs us to pray for our enemies, he is not necessarily speaking of people in distant lands. A spouse can be sharing a bed or a breakfast/dinner table with at least a temporary enemy—one's spouse. Sometimes forgiveness and reconciliation with each other demand commending "the enemy" to healing prayer.

Small Communities Gathered around Marriage Enrichment

Groups of couples who wish to gather regularly around the issues of marriage and family life can contract to focus on one issue per meeting, repeating the issues on a rotating basis. Some of these issues could be:

1. individual responsibility in and for the relationship
2. mutual encouragement
3. individual and shared priorities, values, and game-playing
4. being in touch with one's own feelings
5. listening to and naming one's partner's feelings
6. skills for mutual, shared decision-making
7. conflict resolution

8. communication (as described broadly above) and sexuality
9. reasonable expectations of each other
10. the role of God and faith in the relationship

A marriage and family-life group could certainly add more to the list—for example, addressing some of the same relational issues relative to the children of the family. Such groups, if necessary, need written and then shared dialogue at home between the two spouses on the given issues, one or more times between the meetings of the group. The group-sharing is a sharing of the wisdom and the problems each couple has discovered by working with each other at home. A couple need only share that which they are comfortable sharing. The group dialogue should be set in the context of shared Scripture reading at the beginning of the meeting and spontaneous prayers of petition at the end of the meeting.

I tell couples that the best gift they can give to their children is a strong, loving, marital relationship. That is the key, the cornerstone, to building domestic church at home, or the home as the primal base community. I turn now to some thoughts on how to aid parents in experiencing community with their children.

17

The Faith Community as Training Center for Parenting

In many of these chapters, we, in effect, are saying that society has grown so antirelational that we have to spend time training people in what used to be obvious: how to be neighbor, community, and spousal friend. The same is true with children in a family. There is a growing cry from parents: "teach me how to experience love, community" in my family, with my children. Before we discuss practicalities, let us briefly review the landscape of what it looks and feels like to be a child or teen in today's world.

Dr. Toni Saunders is the director of the Stress Education Center in Evanston, Illinois, and the author of *The Capable Kid Program*, a process designed to teach parents and children stress-management skills. Projecting current trends in the life-style of children and teens onto the year 2000, Dr. Saunders says that a typical class of forty graduating teens will have a profile that looks something like this:

—2 class members will have given birth before graduation;
—8 will have dropped out from school;
—11 will be unemployed after graduation;
—15 will be living in some degree of poverty;
—by graduation, 36 will have used alcohol, 17 marijuana, 8 cocaine;
—6 will have run away;
—1 will have committed suicide.

Dr. Saunders's *futuring* is congruent with what others are saying about the *present*. Dr. David Elkind in *The Hurried Child* speaks of the phenomenon of children under stress, being hurried along and pressured by success-addicted parents. His study of teenagers, *All Grown Up and No Place To Go,* tracks the hurried child into adolescence where the stress is even increased with peer pressure, sexual activity possibilities, drug and alcohol abuse, and a rising suicide rate. Chief among an adolescent's problems is the absence of adult mentoring, guiding, figures. Elkind says most American parents do not have or give time to become markers for their children. A marker is someone you may agree or disagree with, but he or she helps a young person find his or her way in life. Elkind feels two functions that parishes ought to perform on behalf of adolescents are to introduce them to a companion God, who can be spontaneously present to them for support, meaning, and challenge; and to teach adults, especially parents, how to be markers for their young people. Another psychologist, Dr. Stephen Schectman, in an excellent study, *The Missing Link,* writes that one of the key problems facing families of adolescents is the absence of quality time between parent and adolescent child. Dolores Curran has similarly written about the stress affecting modern society.

Saunders, Elkind, Schectman, and Curran provide the motivation for what is to follow. Just as a parish providing marriage enrichment is making an important contribution to the family, becoming the smallest, healthy cell of church, so also providing parents and young people skills for effective relationships with one another similarly helps create domestic church, homes where kingdom values and behavior are practiced.

I believe that every religious education program following the suggestion of the latest foundational documents on evangelization and catechesis, should make parent and family enrichment an ongoing staple of their programming. Specifically some of the following skills ought to be shared with parents especially, adapted to the developmental stages of their children. The list of skills will betray my own graduate training in the vision and skills pioneered by Alfred Adler and Rudolf Dreikurs.

Basic Skills for Effective Parenting and Family Living

I have *adapted* most of these skills for also training children for effective relating in the classroom and in the family. Training can begin in the primary grades.

I. *Active Listening*
When your child says something that encodes feelings, decode the

child's statements into two components: facts and feelings. Show your child that you have heard his/her feelings with a statement like this one: *"When (facts), then you feel (feelings). . . ." Stated either as a declarative sentence or a question, there is always a question implied: "Is this what you are feeling?"*

II. *Confrontation*

Avoid put-down messages, rearrange your confrontation into a description of behavior plus feelings; model such a confrontation on this: *"When (facts—description of behavior) then I feel (describe the feelings the behavior causes in you)."*

III. *Conflicts*

—ineffective method: parent power (child loses)
—ineffective method: child power (parent loses)
—effective method: no-lose, problem solving

1. Identify and define the conflict.
2. Generate possible alternative solutions.
3. Evaluate the alternative solutions.
4. Decide on the best alternative.
5. Work out ways of implementing a solution.
6. Follow up to evaluate how it worked.

All of this is done *together* with the child.

For more enrichment, see Thomas Gordon, *Parent Effectiveness Training* or the Adlerian influenced *Systematic Training for Effective Parenting*.

IV. *Principles from Adlerian Psychology (largely developed by Rudolf Dreikurs)*

A. There is a need for *democratic* families—children and parents who respect the rights and responsibilities of each other.

B. Problematic parenting patterns:

1. *Overindulgent:* the child always gets what it wants; it is brought up to be on the receiving end; it does not want to learn to give in return.
2. *Overpermissive:* not so much concerned with material things; these parents are overconcerned with frustration, and avoiding it.
3. *Overprotective:* the child is raised with a view of the world as "dangerous;" the parent administers lots of don'ts; such children have less contact with other children than others have.
4. *Overdominant:* the parent knows what is good for the child and decides for him or her.

5. *Autocratic:* the parent wields power; he or she verbalizes concern for children; he or she is really concerned about power and self.
C. *Adler-Dreikurs Principles:*
1. *Encouragement*—it should be deliberate; vocal; specific; including demonstration of esteem, affection, appreciation, and step-by-step helping.
2. *Natural consequences*—a situation, the child's decision in the situation, and its natural nonharmful but painful results are used to teach discipline.
3. *Logical consequences*—this involves reasoning with the child that certain behavior will result in a certain course of action.
4. *Action instead of words*—do not homilize; children do not listen.
5. *Take time for training* your children in this new approach to discipline.
6. *Practice firmness, not domination.*
7. *Withdraw from certain games and provocation that children initiate.*
8. *Do not always run to rescue the child (fallacy of first impulses)*—we usually help the child to accomplish his/her goal.
9. *Children and teen's misguided goals, seeking:*
   —special attention
   —power
   —revenge
   —dependency and inadequacy
(When you discern his or her misguided goal, do not engage on the child's field of battle).
10. *Withdrawing from negative provocation, not from the child.*
11. *The importance of having fun together.*
12. *A family council meeting, similar to a family base community meeting, ought to happen:*
   a. at a regular designated hour, once a week;
   b. each family member invited—one vote each if old enough to understand;
   c. decisions may be reached that family members do not like, therefore the value of participating;
   d. not to be used by parents to manipulate—a real experience of democracy;
   e. order and listening are to be practiced;
   f. should be an improvement, solution session;
   g. decisions must be approved by council—endangering, harmful decisions are not even considered;

h. decision should benefit all;

i. nonharmful but nonetheless wrong and unpleasant decisions should be used as an educational experience;

j. as it grows in effectiveness, the family council becomes the family authority;

k. if a child breaks a council agreement, the parent need not feel bound either; no one has a right to change decisions between meetings;

l. be patient—just because sessions might be slow in "catching on" they should not be discontinued.

18

Family-Centered Evangelization and Catechesis

The word *ecology* refers to any interacting system of elements that function holistically toward a total effect. Most frequently we connect the word ecology with the environment. Environmentalists have drilled into our consciousness how disturbing any one part of the environmental ecology has an influence on the whole. Thus, we are now concerned about the hole in the ozone layer that could create a detrimental effect on the environment known as the "greenhouse effect."

In religious education we speak also of an ecology—traditionally there have been pieces functioning together with hoped for results. Specifically, the parochial school and the CCD program have been the main components of the ecology. As we discussed in the andragogy section, heretofore *adults* and *families* have not been included too often in parish religious education ecology. Such an ecology may have functioned well up until the 1960s when neighborhood and family life were relatively stable, supporting, if from a distance, the values and behavior propagated by the school or CCD. The fact is now that the child-centered ecology is not working. The statistics regarding regularly worshiping children, teens, and families are alarming. The child-centered approach is mass-producing the nonpracticing, cultural Catholic. Parochial schools are degenerating into private education, CCD into obligatory "fill my kid with faith" baby-sitting services, which children themselves resent.

Parents must be disabused of the notion that the parochial school or CCD can give their children faith. The ministers and personnel at the school or religious education program are at best "guard wheel" catechists. The real catechists are the parish community itself and the domestic church of the family. If the message perceived at home is that what is

137

presented at school or CCD is not something lived by or practiced in the family, then we have created a religious education schizophrenia—wherein one component of the ecology is delivering one message, but a more basic piece, the family, is delivering another.

Put simply: parishes can no longer afford to homilize parents about how they are the primary religious educators of their children. Because many parents now are either not evangelized themselves or are poorly catechized, we are putting an impossible burden on them. We need to change the educational ecology, building family involvement into the curriculum of parochial school and CCD. Only with such a reshaped ecology will we even create an environment wherein family evangelization and conversion can take place.

Let us look briefly at several models of religious education wherein the educational ecology has shifted to a family-centered one.

1. The New Parish Advantage

The easiest environment to move toward family-centered religious education is a place where a new parish is being formed. Without a tradition or history to deal with, such new faith communities can create the family-centered ecology from the outset.

Two parishes stand out in my mind as excellent examples of this. The first is Spirit of Peace Catholic Community in Longmont, Colorado. The parish is set up as a network of small communities. Some of the base communities invite the children of the adults in the small groups in for a children's session and a family experience every other meeting of the small groups. Other small groups are made up of parents who gather to prepare their children for sacraments. Another parish doing an excellent job along the same lines is Holy Family Parish in Inverness, Illinois, in the archdiocese of Chicago.

2. The Child's Liturgy of the Word Model

Many parishes in the diocese of Richmond, Virginia, and two parishes close to where I live in the suburbs of Chicago, St. Julie's (Tinley Park, Illinois) and Church of the Holy Spirit in Schaumburg are replacing the traditional CCD program with catechesis based on the lectionary, at Sunday Mass. The children are dismissed, for example, at St. Julie's at the liturgy of the word, and go with their Scripture and prayer leader who breaks open the word with them and deals with related catechetical issues. The children join their parents, then, for the liturgy of the eucharist. At Julie's, children's liturgy of the word is being done at almost every Mass on Sunday. A very important dynamic in this model is family worship; it has become normative for involvement in the religious education program.

3. The Traditional Pieces, Rearranged Model

St. John the Evangelist in Streamwood, Illinois, does not have the rooms for dismissal for children's liturgy of the word. Father William Moriarity, Father Gene Dyer, and Sister Kathleen LaPlume have done the next best thing, and turned their 9:30 A.M. Sunday morning Mass into a family Mass ministered by families. Primary, intermediate, and junior high families take turns planning and celebrating. Again *family worship* is a built-in element in this model. Similarly, St. John's has placed preparation for first eucharist and reconciliation on an RCIA-family model. Again, on Sunday morning, families meet on a semiregular basis for breakfast. Then adults are engaged in adult catechesis, the children in children's catechesis. The sixty-minute session closes with a family experience, and then group worship at the 11:00 A.M. Sunday eucharist.

In both the 9:30 family Mass and the 9:30 A.M. family education/11:00 A.M. Mass models, school *and* CCD families are involved, thus removing the wall that often exists between these two vehicles of religious education.

At Holy Comforter-St. Cyprian in Washington, D.C., Father Ray Kemp and his staff annually hold the minicatechumenate on the Monday evenings of Lent. It is for all families preparing for first communion, reconciliation, and confirmation. Similar to St. John's, adults receive adult catechesis and children are ministered to separately by catechists. Parents and children join at the end of the night for a family experience. The model has become so popular that families do not mind repeating the process with younger children who become ready for a sacramental moment.

At St. Hubert's, a parish I served in for seven years, we started some of the processes now being used at St. John's. Fr. Bill Moriarity, who served with me at St. Hubert's, brought the family emphasis with him when he became pastor at St. John's. An additional thing we did at St. Hubert's was to annually interview all parents involved in parochial school and CCD. It was a huge undertaking that involved the whole staff interviewing parents in groups of ten or so. In the interviews, we solicited their reaction to the parish, their needs to be addressed by future ministries, and explained our rationale for our heavily familial emphasis. At the time there were over seven hundred children in the school and over thirteen hundred in the religious education (CCD) program. The interview gave us the opportunity to explain effective religious education as involving parish staff-catechist-family collaboration. We metaphorically spoke of this collaboration as the "love triangle" that must exist if our children are to have faith.

Please note that at St. John's, Holy Comforter-St. Cyprian's, and St. Hubert's the traditional elements of school and CCD were maintained, but family involvement was shot through into every grade level, not just sacramental preparation years.

To return to one of the original themes of this book: *realizing family evangelization and catechesis is a necessity.* Parish leaders need to use their *imagination,* as these parishes have, to mainstream family involvement in religious education.

Conclusion

Though these final chapters on family consciousness, ministry to marriage, ministry to parents and family life, and family-centered evangelization and catechesis have been presented in separate chapters, the reader should not see these as segregated pieces, one or two of which a parish may choose to experiment with, smorgasbord style. In fact, each one of them is a vital piece of what should be a holistic, integrated ecology and discipline, that effectively re-imagines the parish around family life. In some way, all these elements must be attempted if families are going to be ministered to well. Each segment builds upon and is connected to the others.

19
So Now . . .

As Rosemary Blueher, director of small communities for the diocese of Joliet, and I concluded a recent workshop on small communities, I walked to the chalkboard in silence and wrote the following words on the board (I heard people saying them, repeating them slowly as I wrote): "So now, go home, and use your imagination!" I want to close this book in a similar way. Go now . . . use your imagination.

I have tried through these pages to interweave theory/theology and models that are being lived in pastoral-parish settings. In the interweaving I have tried to refrain, especially in the presentation of models, from implying "You ought to do things in the same way." No, I have tried only to present theory and models to stimulate your imagination. We have tried to look at the future of parish life through three dominant images, heretofore underdeveloped by many American mainline churches: small communities, adulthood and adult faith, and family life. I have suggested that these three images are the key to the future growth and evangelization of any church, specifically the Roman Catholic Church. But you, the reader—either as an individual or in communion with brothers and sisters concerned about your parish—you are the experts concerning your local church. Use the theory, study the models, bounce them against your own wisdom and experience, and come up with models of small groups, ministry to adults, and ministries with a family consciousness that are better than any I have devised or the others mentioned in this book. This book is, in effect, a consultant, bringing you pictures of things others have done or are doing. The creative burden is on you and your imagination to bring what I have presented and other input you may have in these matters to bear on the reality of your parish, and adapt models, create new models that better fit your local situation.

141

Keep in mind how imagination functions. Sometimes after wading through layers of material like this book, a person needs to close the book, put it away, suspend judgment and action for a while, and allow the imagination time to assimilate and project forward into the future, or the possible, or the probable. Sometimes intuition or insight comes as a result of distance or getting away from the issues at hand. Even if we are trying to get away from, or distance ourselves from, these three issues, if they are important to us, they will remain *with us* and *within us* on the level of the preconscious or subconscious. The imagination will be functioning, firing subliminally. Walk away from the issues of this book for a while. If you really care about what we have shared about, new thoughts, feelings, and images will begin to emerge despite your distancing.

Sometimes the imagination cries out, not for distance, but for more input, to literally be immersed more deeply in wisdom and information. If that is where you find yourself now, I hope the models, the other authors named, the bibliography, the sites and addresses help you to begin a journey of deepening your wisdom more and more in these three areas. For some persons, the imagination cries out, after a taste of some information, for more and more. The deeper immersion into issues, the more concentrated study of and reflection on issues, results in the firing of the deeper levels of the imagination. Sometimes imagination has to "get away from it;" sometimes imagination has to "get more into it."

Sometimes, whether in distance or immersion, the imagination functions to synthesize—to pull a few key insights or strategies from a complex mixture of material or experiences, to extract common denominators, or threads running through apparently diverse notions, or compartmentalized issues or experiences. Perhaps the three dominant images of this book—communities, adulthood, and family—will project on the screen of some of your imaginations one *new* or *renewed dominant image* that will begin to influence your faith or your ministry.

Both Philip Keane and Richard Gula are priests and moral theologians for whom I have much respect and admiration. They have begun to write and speak a great deal on the importance of the imagination in moral development and conscience formation. For years we have stressed in the Catholic Church the rational principles in making conscience decisions. Keane, Gula, and others have begun to discover that while the importance of reasoning and principles will never go away, a great deal of individual and collective morality and conscience is determined by imagination and the dominant images within and around us. Reflecting on their research, I have come to discover that a great deal of moral behavior is influenced by the interacting of personal, intrapsychic/spiritual, dominant images; cultural dominant images; and faith tradition-ecclesial dominant images. Morality, healthy or not so healthy, is heavily influenced by the interacting of several levels of dominant images.

In much the same way, in striving for parishes that facilitate adult conversion, domestic church, small cell groups, all of which contribute toward a healthier *ecclesia,* let domiant images from several strata interact with each other until there is the birthing of new dominant images. Allow intrapersonal dominant images to collide with interpersonal images collectively shared. Allow these to collide with the dominant images of the culture, and also the dominant images of status quo ecclesiology and pastoral praxis. Let all of this bear down on the issues and reality of parish life. Collectively pray for wisdom and discernment. Slowly new images of parish will emerge. As they do, make them goals. As they become goals, create time-lines and action plans. Never give up. There is not so much failure as there is learning from evaluating, then reshaping, and trying again.

Try it. You will see, if you have not already. Imagination is the prophetic artist of the future. What you imagined will become reality. Others will then institutionalize it. It will then begin to lose passion. Then it will be time to re-imagine all over again. *Imagination:* such a great gift, such a holy gift. Thank you, Lord!

Appendix

Father Thomas Maney's (et al) *Parish Neighborhood Renewal Ministry* can be contacted through:
Mrs. Anna Chernugal
PNRM
1950 25th Street
Hibbing, MN 55746
(218) 262-2482

Father Michael Eivers and Rev. Mr. A. Perry Vitale can be reached for more information on the OIKOS model at:
St. Boniface Catholic Church
8330 Johnson Street
Pembrooke Pines, FL 33024
(305) 432-2750

Little Rock Scripture Study Materials and Inservice can be obtained through:
Little Rock Scripture Study
The Liturgical Press
St. John's Abbey
Collegeville, MN 56321
(612) 363-2213

Parish Spiritual, ed. by Father Patrick Brennan can be obtained via the Office for Chicago Catholic Evangelization at the following address:
Office for Chicago Catholic Evangelization
Archdiocese of Chicago
Post Office Box 1979
Chicago, IL 60690
(312) 751-8319

Bibliography

Ad Hoc Committee on Marriage and Family Life, National Conference of Catholic Bishops. *A Family Perspective in Church and Society: A Manual for All Pastoral Leaders*. Washington, DC: United States Catholic Conference, 1988.

Baranowski, Arthur C. *Creating Small Faith Communities*. Cincinnati, OH: St. Anthony Messenger Press, 1988.

———. *Pastoring the Pastors*. Cincinnati, OH: St. Anthony Messenger Press, 1988.

Baranowski, Arthur C., with Kathleen M. O'Reilly and Carrie M. Prio. *Praying Alone and Together*. Cincinnati, OH: St. Anthony Messenger Press, 1988.

Barry, William A., and William J. Connolly. *The Practice of Spiritual Direction*. New York: Seabury, 1982.

Bellah, Robert N., Richard Madsen, William M. Sullivan, Ann Swidler, and Steven M. Tipton. *Habits of the Heart*. Berkeley and Los Angeles: University of California Press, 1985.

Boff, Leonardo. *Church: Charism, and Power*. New York: Crossroad, 1985.

———. *Ecclesiogenesis*. Maryknoll, NY: Orbis, 1986.

Brennan, Patrick J. *The Evangelizing Parish*. Allen, TX: Tabor Publishing, 1987.

———. *Penance and Reconciliation*. Chicago: Thomas More, 1986.

Brewi, Janice, and Anne Brennan. *Celebrate Mid-Life: Jungian Archetypes and Mid-Life Spirituality*. New York: Crossroad, 1988.

———. *Mid-Life: Psychological and Spiritual Perspectives*. New York: Crossroad, 1982.

Burnside, Irene. *Working with the Elderly: Group Process and Techniques*. Boston, MA: Jones and Bartlett, 1986.

Cappellaro, Juan Bautista. *From a Crowd to the People of God*. Rome: Better World Movement, 1983.

147

Christensen, Oscar C., and Thomas G. Schramski. *Adlerian Family Counseling.* Minneapolis: Educational Media Corp., 1983.

Clark, Stephen B. *Building Christian Communities.* Notre Dame, IN: Ave Maria Press, 1972.

Cook, Paul, and Judith Zeiler. *Neighborhood Ministry Basics: A No-nonsense Guide.* Washington, DC: Pastoral Press, 1986.

Cowan, Michael A., James D. Whitehead, Evelyn Easton Whitehead, David N. Power, O.M.I., and John Shea. *Alternatives for Worship.* Collegeville, MN: Liturgical Press, 1987.

Cox, Harvey. *The Silencing of Leonardo Boff.* Oak Park, IL: Meyer-Stone, 1988.

Curran, Dolores. *Stress and the Healthy Family.* Minneapolis: Winston Press, 1985.

———. *Traits of a Healthy Family.* Minneapolis: Winston Press, 1983.

Deck, Allan Figueroa, S.J. *The Second Wave.* Mahwah, NJ: Paulist Press, 1989.

Diocese of Little Rock. *The Little Rock Scripture Study.* Collegeville, MN: Liturgical Press, 1986.

Donovan, Vincent J. *Christianity Rediscovered.* Maryknoll, NY: Orbis, 2nd ed., 1982.

Dreikurs, Rudolf, M.D. *Children: The Challenge.* New York: Hawthorn Books, 1964.

Dychtwald, Ken, and Joe Flower. *Age Wave: The Challenges and Opportunities of an Aging America.* Los Angeles: Jeremy P. Tarcher, 1989.

Elkind, David. *All Grown Up and No Place To Go.* Reading, MA: Addison-Wesley, 1984.

———. *The Hurried Child.* Reading, MA: Addison-Wesley, 1981.

Foltz, Nancy T. *Handbook of Adult Religious Education.* Birmingham, AL: Religious Education Press, 1986.

Ford, Iris M. *Life Spiral: The Faith Journey.* Burlington, Ontario: Welch, 1988.

Freire, Paulo. *Pedagogy of the Oppressed.* New York: Continuum, 1970.

Furlong, J. Daryl. *The Ministry of Listening: Ministering with a Family Perspective.* Chicago: Buckley Publications, 1987.

The Gallup Organization. *The Unchurched American.* Princeton, NJ: Gallup Organization, 1988.

Gilligan, Carol. *In a Different Voice: Psychological Theory and Women's Development.* Cambridge, MA: Harvard University Press, 1982.

Gilmour, Peter. *The Emerging Pastor: Non-ordained Catholic Pastors.* Kansas City, MO: Sheed and Ward, 1986.

Gordon, Thomas. *P.E.T. Parent Effectiveness Training.* New York: Plume, 1970.

———. *T.E.T. Teacher Effectiveness Training.* New York: Hyden, 1974.

Griffin, Emilie. *Turning.* Garden City, NY: Doubleday, 1980.

Hammett, Rosine, C.S.C., and Loughlan Sofield, S.T. *Inside Christian Community.* New York: Le Jacq Publishing, 1981.

Harris, Maria. *Teaching and Religious Imagination.* San Francisco: Harper & Row, 1987.

Hoge, Dean. *Converts, Drop-Outs, and Returnees.* New York: Pilgrim Press, 1981.

Hoffman, Virginia. *Birthing a Living Church.* New York: Crossroad, 1988.

Hubbard, Most Rev. Howard. "Developing a Family Perspective in Society and the Church," in *Origins* 15, no. 19 (October 24, 1985). National Catholic News Service, Washington, DC.

Hurston, John. *Home Fellowships International Training Manual.* Dallas: Word of Faith Publisher, 1986.

Hurston, John W., and Karen L. Hurston. *Caught in the Web.* Church Growth International: Mountain Press, 1977.

International Commission on English in the Liturgy and Bishops' Committee on the Liturgy. *Rite of Christian Initiation of Adults: Study Edition.* Chicago: Liturgy Training Publications, 1988.

Kegan, Robert. *The Evolving Self.* Cambridge: Harvard University Press, 1982.

Keane, Philip S., S.S. *Christian Ethics and Imagination.* Ramsey, NJ: Paulist Press, 1984.

Kennedy, Eugene. *Tomorrow's Catholics, Yesterday's Church.* New York: Harper & Row, 1988.

Knowles, Malcolm S. *The Modern Practice of Adult Education: From Pedagogy to Andragogy.* Chicago: Follett, 1980.

Kolbenschlag, Madonna. *Lost in the Land of Oz.* San Francisco: Harper & Row, 1988.

Lee, Bernard J., and Michael A. Cowan. *Dangerous Memories.* Kansas City, MO: Sheed and Ward, 1986.

Levinson, Daniel J., with Charlotte N. Darrow, Edward B. Klein, Maria H. Levinson, and Braxton McKee. *The Seasons of a Man's Life.* New York: Alfred A. Knopf, 1978.

Lobinger, F. *Towards Non-dominating Leadership: Aims and Methods of the Lumko Series*. Lady Frere, Netherlands: Lumko Institute, 1986.

Loder, James E. *The Transforming Moment*. San Francisco: Harper & Row, 1981.

Martos, Joseph. *Doors to the Sacred*. Garden City, NY: Doubleday, 1981.

May, Gerald G., M.D. *Addiction and Grace*. San Francisco: Harper & Row, 1988.

McKenzie, Leon. *The Religious Education of Adults*. Birmingham, AL: Religious Education Press, 1982.

Murphy, Sheila M. *Midlife Wanderer: The Woman Religious in Midlife Transition*. Natick, MA: Affirmation Books, 1983.

National Advisory Committee on Adult Education, "Adult Religious Education and the American Catholic Family," in *Origins* 15, no. 23 (November 21, 1985). National Catholic News Service, Washington, DC.

O'Meara, Thomas Franklin, O.P. *Theology of Ministry*. Ramsey, NJ: Paulist Press, 1983.

Parks, Sharon. *The Critical Years*. San Francisco: Harper & Row, 1986.

Pope Paul VI. *Evangelii Nuntiandi*. Washington, DC: United States Catholic Conference, 1975.

Schaef, Anne Wilson. *When Society Becomes an Addict*. San Francisco: Harper & Row, 1987.

Schaef, Anne Wilson, and Diane Fassel. *The Addictive Organization*. San Francisco: Harper & Row, 1988.

Senior, Donald, C.P., and Carroll Stuhlmueller, O.P. *The Biblical Foundations for Mission*. Maryknoll, NY: Orbis, 1983.

Shechtman, Stephen Allen, and Mark J. Singer. *The Missing Link: Building Quality Time with Teens*. Nashville: Abingdon Press, 1985.

Shulman, Bernard H., M.D., and Raeann Berman. *Surviving Your Aging Parents*. Chicago: Surrey Books, 1988.

Smith, Cynthia S. *The Seven Levels of Marriage*. Secaucus, NJ: Lyle Stuart, 1986.

Stokes, Kenneth, ed., with Malcolm Knowles, Winston Gooden, Mary Wilcox, Gabriel Moran, and James Fowler. *Faith Development in the Adult Life Cycle*. New York: W. H. Sadlier, 1982.

Studzinski, Raymond, O.S.B. *Spiritual Direction and Mid-Life Development*. Chicago: Loyola University Press, 1985.

Synod of Bishops. *The Evangelization of the Modern World*. Washington, DC: United States Catholic Conference, 1973.

Wallis, Jim. *The Call to Conversion.* San Francisco: Harper & Row, 1981.

Warren, Michael. *Source Book for Modern Catechetics.* Winona, MN: St. Mary's Press, 1983.

Welch, Sharon D. *Communities of Resistance and Solidarity: A Feminist Theology of Liberation.* Maryknoll, NY.: Orbis, 1985.